THE MEASUREMENT OF PROFIT

THE MEASUREMENT
OF PROFIT

BY

F. SEWELL BRAY

*Senior Nuffield Research Fellow
in the Department of Applied Economics
Cambridge*

GEOFFREY CUMBERLEGE
OXFORD UNIVERSITY PRESS
LONDON   NEW YORK   TORONTO
1949

Oxford University Press, Amen House, London, E.C.4

GLASGOW   NEW YORK   TORONTO   MELBOURNE   WELLINGTON
BOMBAY   CALCUTTA   MADRAS   CAPE TOWN

Geoffrey Cumberlege, Publisher to the University

PRINTED IN ENGLAND BY
HAZELL, WATSON & VINEY Lᴛᴅ
LONDON AND AYLESBURY

PREFACE

LITTLE need be said by way of introduction to a book by Mr. Bray on a subject so central to the interest of accountants and economists as the Measurement of Profit. While principally concerned here with the present position of accounting thought on the subject and the modifications of existing technical procedures which seem to him desirable, Mr. Bray endeavours throughout to view the position from the standpoint of the economist as well as the accountant. The result of this approach may be illustrated in the following way.

If the ideas of accountants and economists on the subject of, say, the proper definition and classification of the transactions represented in a set of business accounting statements are compared, they seem to be in close accord, except on two main issues : provision for depreciation and inventory valuation. Both these issues are highly complex and have long been the subject of debate among both economists and accountants though, until recently, all too little between the two groups. The two approaches have inevitably been different. The accountant has naturally been chiefly concerned with practical issues viewed first and foremost from the standpoint of proprietorship interests and many of his principles appear to date from a time when money was, or at least was thought to be, more or less stable in value. The economist on the other hand has not been haunted in the same way by day to day problems and their practical solution and consequently has been in a more favourable position to develop ideal concepts and principles without too much regard for the details of their practical application. At present the possibility of such academic aloofness is fast disappearing from many economists with the rapid development of national income and social accounting studies. At the same time the obvious instability of money values over the past generation, the present high rates of taxation and the growing stress on the contribution of businesses to the national welfare has led some accountants to question traditional procedures however well they may have served their purpose in the past. The interplay and as far as may be reconciliation of these two points of view is everywhere apparent in this work.

Much of the work of this inquiry was undertaken at the Department of Applied Economics. In view however of the general interest of the accountancy profession in this subject the present arrangements were made for publication.

RICHARD STONE.

CAMBRIDGE.
June, 1949.

The Author extends to Authors and Publishers of all works from which quotations have been taken, to the Institute of Chartered Accountants in England and Wales, the Society of Incorporated Accountants and Auditors and the Controller of H.M. Stationery Office his thanks for their kind co-operation in granting permission to quote extracts from their publications.

CONTENTS

Preface by J. R. N. STONE, Director of the Department of
Applied Economics in the University of Cambridge .. p. v

Acknowledgement .. .. p. viii

Chapter I—Introduction 1

II—The Nature of Income and Capital 10

III—The Nature of Profit 37

" Lord Beaconsfield, in one of his novels, has defined a practical man as a man who practises the errors of his forefathers. The Romans were a great race, but they were cursed with the sterility which waits upon practicality. They did not improve upon the knowledge of their forefathers, and all their advances were confined to the minor technical details of engineering. They were not dreamers enough to arrive at new points of view, which could give a more fundamental control over the forces of nature."

An Introduction to Mathematics by A. N. Whitehead, pp. 40–41 (Oxford, 1945).

ACKNOWLEDGEMENT

During the years 1946 to 1948 I was a member of a joint advisory sub-committee of accountants and economists, presided over by Mr. Stone, which was set up by a Joint Exploratory Committee representing the Institute of Chartered Accountants in England and Wales and the National Institute of Economic and Social Research. In a number of respects this book is based on, and anticipates the publication of, a report on accounting terms and concepts in the drafting of which I participated and which is still under consideration by the Joint Exploratory Committee. I would like to acknowledge the mental stimulus and benefit I received from my colleagues on the advisory sub-committee without of course committing the sub-committee or either of the convening organisations to any of the views that appear in this book.

It will also be apparent that this book owes much to other people's work. In all cases I have sought to indicate the source of such material by the use of precise footnote references. It is always possible however that by some mischance an acknowledgement may have been overlooked. If such is the case the acknowledgement is no less sincere, the omission will have been quite unintentional and I hope may be forgiven.

F. S. B.

I

INTRODUCTION[1]

ACCOUNTING is the art of recording, classifying and summarising in terms of units of money the many and diverse economic transactions which day by day enter into the business affairs of society. It is intimately associated with business enterprise and this is the implication which is sought by the use of the expression private accounting first suggested by Mr. J. R. Hicks to distinguish the accounting of the individual firm from the accounting of the whole community or nation.[2] As one might expect accounting is a utilitarian art based on conventions, and nowhere is this more apparent than in its efforts to measure business profits. Accounting methods are very largely judged acceptable in proportion to their usefulness in assessing profit margins in relation to the conduct and management of business enterprise.

The plain recording function of accounting is a technical matter, the mechanics of which need give little trouble to the trained accountant. The analytical, epitomising, and interpretive functions of accounting rest on a higher plane and call for penetrating qualities of judgment and perception. They are mainly directed to the service of two ends, the one a report of stewardship designed in such a manner as to be understood by those persons who neither specialise in accounts nor necessarily take part in business management ; the other a report of operational progress so ordered as to assist executives in the efficient running of business.

In a free enterprise economy the measurement of profit is a major consideration. In a controlled economy the conventions appropriate to private enterprise accounting may lose something of their force or change their direction to accord with the new kind of incentives sought for the well-being of society. There is nothing necessarily static about the nature of accounting conventions once it is recognised that they are accommodated to those uses of accounts which current social and economic concepts require. In comparatively recent times the divorce between ownership and management in the conduct of business

[1] The substance of this introduction first appeared in the form of a paper, read at Leicester in July, 1947, on the occasion of the Jubilee of the foundation of the Leicester Colleges of Art and Technology. It was afterwards published under the title of " The Measurement of Profit " in *The Accountant* dated 12th and 19th July, 1947.

[2] *The Social Framework*, p. vi. (Oxford, 1942).

within the constitutional framework of the limited liability company has imposed legal constraints framed to ensure that published accounting reports adequately disclose to proprietorship interests the achievements of those responsible for carrying out the objects of the enterprise in relation to the preservation of contributed money capital, and the distribution of dividends out of earned profits.

As things are, the concept of profit as a money residue between cost inputs and revenue outputs arising from the performance of business operations is at the very heart of current accounting practice. In the circumstances of the future it may become rather less a measure of money incentive to ownership and rather more a measure of stability to society in the sense of savings utilised to the purpose of asset formation. In this context the measurement of savings is cardinal for we know that whenever outlay on fixed equipment is out of line with current savings out of income, then disruptive forces are set in motion prejudicial to the long run evenness of business enterprise.

In this book, then, we shall take this central concept of profit measurement as fundamental to private accounting practice, we shall look at it in terms of money flows, and we shall seek to state the implications which arise when those money flows are related to the passage of the goods and services which pass against them. We shall look at the currently accepted conventions of accounting practice and we shall try to see why they grew up in their present form and to test their validity in a world of change.

Private accounting as we understand it to-day is a relatively modern art, and the profession to which it has given rise is comparatively new. Nevertheless within the short span of its existence in an organised form this profession has been called upon to shoulder a wide range of practical duties, and many of the day to day problems of the professional accountant have had to be solved in a business setting in which expedient issues have exerted the more pressing claims. Not unnaturally accountants have felt their responsibilities to lie at the money end of things, and accounting theory has largely taken for granted a quality of stability in the monetary unit. Thus it comes about that private accounting practice wears an historical air so that the term value is very largely coterminous with money cost ; historical costs and historical revenues lie at the very foundation of accounting technique.

Accrual and expiry accounting, with its firm insistence on the temporal element in the preparation of accounts, has not infrequently imposed the strain of adjustment in unsuspected periods of sharp technical change, so that quite apart from price variations even historical measurements of profit have not been altogether free from some distortion though consistency *was* the ideal sought.

The accounting document which sets out to display profit measurement is known in England as the profit and loss account, and in

America more commonly as the income statement. Its main purpose is to give a fair and reasonable indication of the operational earning ability of a business enterprise under the conditions existing during the accounting period to which it is related as determined by a consistent application of acceptable methods. It cannot be too strongly emphasised that such an accounting measurement has been looked upon from the standpoint of the individual firm ; it has been conceived in terms of a money margin and by the nature of the reasons which have brought it into being there has been but slight understanding of the social and economic implications which might attach to such a measurement, unless it be that a regard for the protection of proprietors and creditors and a concern for the claims of the Inland Revenue are held to constitute a sufficient penetration into such implications. For some of us it was never more than the fringe of the matter, and it is not difficult to conjecture far-reaching developments in the accounting technique of profit measurement just so soon as economic conceptions are fully comprehended in their depth both by men of business and their accounting advisers. A well sought concept of profit measurement deduced from such a background will make its own contribution to a course setting which looks to the well-being of the community for its aim.

As a convenient tool of business enterprise accounting technique has been intimately associated with the practice of business men. It is but a commonplace to remind the reader that throughout the greater run of trade and commerce business men have thought of monetary gain as a measure of their success. Anyone with a close experience of business will know the degree of reliance which is placed on the realised monetary increment which results from a successful deal. We are all familiar with the view that a good business man is one who makes money and although it is possible to trace this outlook from the days of simple merchanting transactions it has never ceased to colour all types and developments of industrial enterprise. It was but to be expected that accounting technique should mirror this view and such we shall find it both in the evolution of its forms and in its standards of measurement. Money is the basis and unit of account, and in the past accounting as the tool of business has not unnaturally seen its purpose in records of money making. Its deeper mission of bringing into play the quantifiable and measurable qualities of its art in the service of economic effectiveness, whether it be that of the individual firm or the community, it is only just but now aware. With the burden of portrayal of money-making accounting theory sought to find relative certainty in the practice of conservatism, understatement was preferred to overstatement in the valuation of assets, and in order to safeguard the proprietary of income distribution the recognition of profit was delayed until actual realisation in terms of cash or its

3

equivalent. There was much in this approach which was inherently sound so far as concerned the stability of the individual enterprise and we shall need to look very closely at its methods and aims before we seek to suggest any variations which may seem to depart from its principle. It will involve an inquiry into the whole process of matching the money costs of a continuing business with its money revenues, and this will bring us to the point at which it will become necessary to look at that foundational accounting concept—cost of sales.

At this stage in our investigation we shall be led on to one of the most fundamental problems associated with the accounting measurement of profit—the problem of the method of valuation of inventories of the unused materials, the work in progress or process, and the unsold finished goods in existence at the beginning and the ending of the time period for which a profit measure is sought. It is obvious to business men no less than accountants and economists that assessments of business profits may mean much or little in proportion to the care which has been bestowed upon the valuation of inventories. In this context the choice of method and the accuracy with which it has been carried out play a prominent part. We shall look at methods of valuation of unconverted and partly converted materials from the internal standpoint of the individual firm, in the hope that it may throw some further light upon those difficult questions of unrecovered costs which arise at the close of the time interval constituted by an accounting period, the source and time of profit and the degree of emphasis to be placed on the one or other of these concepts, and the compromises to which accountants resort in particular cases. We shall be called upon to examine the distinction between fixed and moving costs in rather more detail than has been the wont of accountants in the past. We shall find that this distinction raises some fundamental issues when it comes to questions of cost recovery in relation to internal accounting statements designed to test the effectiveness of conversion operations. Again, it will be necessary to consider the money measurement of those finished goods which because they are unsold at the date of account take their place in the inventory valuations, and more especially must we view this question in circumstances which are such that current market value is of greater significance than unrecovered cost. At this stage a critical examination of a long accepted inventory valuation tenet of accounting theory—cost or lower market value—should come as no surprise.

Mr. G. O. May, a leading American accountant, has said that a " growing recognition of the importance of accounting is bound to result in closer examination of the relation between accounting and economics, a subject that has not as yet received very extended consideration." He goes on to give it as his opinion that " accounting is a tool of business, and that the development of accounting, like the development of business law, has been determined by the practices of businessmen. Where accounting and economic thought are found to run along parallel lines, it is probable that both will be found to be running parallel to good business practice. Where accounting treatment diverges from economic theory, a similar divergence is likely to be found between economic theory and business practice ".[1] For ourselves we are tempted to read into these comments the suggestion of a standard of good business practice which should delimit the paths of theoretical accounting and economic developments, but, as we have observed, the business man tends rather to respond to motives which are governed by monetary considerations. The economist, on the other hand, has not forgotten the origin of his subject in the moral sciences and he sets out to formulate his concepts by looking behind the monetary machinery of the world of business with a view to discovering the first principles of an economy of real resources and in this connotation he is much concerned with the stability of the productive effectiveness of the individual enterprise in relation to the material well-being of the community. No one should doubt that inclinations of such an order are central to the solution of problems associated with the measurement of profit, and in so far as economists are successful in deducing concepts which may be brought into application for the betterment of those engaged in the business of society there is an implied obligation on the accounting art to carry them into its own theoretical background. By such comprehension it may promote the penetration of economic concepts into the ways of business by giving to them a practical turn in the shape of quantifiably measurable expressions.

But if we seem to accentuate the case for an extension of economic concepts to the practice of accounting there is also the other side of the picture. Financial accounts, as now drafted with a regard for design and accuracy of statement, set forth the important effects of purely monetary considerations on the little economy of an enterprise which a too rigorous adherence to *real* concepts might tend to overlay, and accountants are not necessarily so wide of the mark, as we might be tempted into thinking, when they sense that their profit and loss accounts do give an institutional indication of money savings while their balance sheets, within the limits of accounting conventions, can and do show something of what has happened to those money savings by way of asset formation and its concomitant liquidity preference.

The extension of traditional functions of government has been within the immediate experience of most of us, and accountants have seen their forms of account brought into use not only as instruments in the assessment of taxation—that is familiar enough—but as a means of regulating prices. Such uses in themselves must impel us to seek

[1] G. O. May, *Twenty-five Years of Accounting Responsibility* 1911–1936, p. 305 (American Institute Publishing Co.).

appropriate concepts and appropriate measurements in the statement of business accounts, but there is still more to be reckoned with. The application of double-entry accounting forms to the difficult task of making quantitative calculations of the relative strengths of the different economic forces operative in the nation is slowly making some headway and may well become an essential piece of machinery in the hands of central governments concerned to promote a policy of general economic welfare.[1] In this context it may be remarked that Marshall who achieved so much by the methods of qualitative economic analysis was himself led to feel the pressing necessity for an overall analysis in quantitative terms as a means to further decisions beneficial to the national economy in the immediate and less immediate futures. To an age which has left the philosophy of laisser-faire far behind the pressure of necessity is but the more urgent and calculations of national aggregates for income, expenditure, saving, asset formation, capital and the like, take on a significance far beyond that thought appropriate to an era in which equilibrium was but the natural handmaid of a developing order. In the last resort social accounts are very largely a combination of private accounts whatever may be their present statistical derivation and if the whole is to present a fair and reasonable working picture over a given time period it is clear that the primary parts constituted by the mass and variety of private accounts must be set on lines which make for requirements of uniformity and consistency. Such requirements do but reinforce the accounting need of right concepts—economic no less than accounting—proper monetary measurements, unambiguous terminology, clear designs, and adequate disclosures in the presentation of accounting forms, all of which are peculiarly relevant to the statement of income generation through the medium of the profit and loss account. There is still a secondary point to be touched upon. If the transfer of some particular facilities of production from private to public ownership is held to engender social welfare then accounting forms should minister to the disposition of its economic tests in the pattern of quantitative measurements of the social benefits, or if it be not too unseemly to add, the social costs inherent in the transfer.

In this discussion some of the more particular effects of accounting profit measurement will not have passed unnoticed. The profit and loss account is useful to the proprietors of an enterprise because it tells them the amount of money profit which they have realised from all those sources of possible income—e.g. by the operational user of assets, by security or property investment and so on—which they tapped during the currency of a given period of account. This

[1] Cf. The Social Accounts of the United Kingdom first included as Appendix V to the White Paper on national income and expenditure of the United Kingdom 1938 to 1946, Cmd. 7099.

institutionally aggregate measure of money profit when considered against the background of past profit accumulations (positive or negative) discloses the limits of current income distribution. That is to say by relation to current asset resources it calls up an executive decision as to what proportion of the profit fund shall be distributed to proprietors either by way of dividends or withdrawals, and what proportion shall be reserved to the oncoming period or periods of account as savings. As accountants well know this executive decision cannot be made without due regard for the legal constraints on income distribution imposed by company law and the financial constraints imposed by the borders of insolvency, but when that decision has been made it is clearly one of great consequence to proprietorship investors both present and prospective, and profit and loss accounts, which have been prepared with an eye to the careful measurement of profit and which are so published that the means employed to the ascertainment of that measurement are adequately disclosed, must promote such a status to organised asset yields that movements of capital are assisted into right channels.[1]

[1] Cambridge economists will recall that Professor Pigou in his discussion of the "hindrances to equality of returns, due to imperfect knowledge" has the following comments on business accounting. "First, it must be observed that the returns, which are important as a guide to the right distribution of resources, are those that are accruing in different uses from resources turned into them at each successive moment. The quotient obtained by dividing the net income of a business by the sum of all the money investment made in it in the past would, in a stationary state, afford a true measure of the returns to current investment there. But in actual conditions the measure thus obtained will often be hopelessly misleading. For example, a man may have put £100,000 into a factory for making some particular thing, and the factory may have been destroyed by fire or may have become worthless through obsolescence. An investment of £10,000 now might have just yielded him a return of £2,000, or 20 per cent. on the new investment, but the return on the total investment will appear as £2,000 on £110,000, or less than 2 per cent. This sort of difficulty could hardly fail to obscure relevant facts however excellently business accounts were drawn up and however fully they were published.
The next thing that calls for comment is the general character of the accounts as they actually are. In businesses conducted by private firms no statement of profits is made public. In businesses conducted by joint stock companies a certain amount of publicity is enforced by law. But stock-watering and other devices are often used to conceal from outsiders the rate of return that is obtained on the capital actually invested, so that, even when this would afford a reasonable guide to the return on current investment, and, therefore, to future prospects, the way is blocked to anybody other than a specialist. The difficulty is still further enhanced by the fact that the prospects which it is necessary to forecast refer, not to immediate returns only, but to returns spread over a considerable period. It is evident that, as regards these returns, even correct knowledge of the immediate past gives but imperfect guidance. . . . Nevertheless, there is clearly room for improvement in the matter of business publicity, and, if such improvements were made, ignorance would be lessened, equality in the values of marginal net products promoted, and the size of the national dividend consequently increased." (*The Economics of Welfare*, pp. 149–151, Fourth Edition Reprinted, Macmillan, 1946.)

Financial accounting documents have an important bearing on grants of credit facilities to business enterprises. A past ability to earn realised money profits, as evidenced by a firm's profit and loss accounts, in relation to money capitals employed, as evidenced by a firm's balance sheets, is not infrequently a major issue which guides the lower level advance policies of banks and such-like financial institutions. Although we may have to consider how far the relationship between money profit and money capital employed, within the context of existing conventions, is a valid test of the effective user of organised assets, there is no doubt as to its relevance to current banking practice. Ability to earn a profit is thought of as promoting an ability to save money, a proposition easily comprehended by institutions whose principal function it is to deal in money claims. Nevertheless a firm which has not yet attained to its optimum output within the conditions it operates, may be forced to utilise its savings out of realised profits in acquiring extended facilities of production, in which case the grantor of credit will at least have additional cover to back his original advance. Money capital employed will rise in relation to money borrowed, thereby slackening the degree of risk carried by the lender. On the other hand there is a presumption that savings out of realised profits will be constituted by an increase in the borrower's current resources in which case the accounting conditions are such that the original advance should be capable of displaying that essential British banking quality—self-liquidation.[1]

But there is another issue arising from accounting measurements of money profits, in particular the money profits of public companies whose stocks and/or shares are quoted on recognised Stock Exchanges, which bears mention here. In the business world realised money profits have come to be regarded, rightly or wrongly, as approximate measures of earning *capacity ;* future trends are almost subconsciously inferred from past results, sometimes even without a proper regard for changing circumstances. Prospective investors reveal a propensity to mirror this view with the consequence that current values of proprietorship rights in institutional capitals tend to be judged by conventional multipliers of realised yields, as qualified by actual distributions. In this context it is not difficult to see the far-reaching influence of accounting profit measurements of public corporate bodies as soon as security valuations are made to depend on earning capacities, for in times of confidence and rising prosperity such valuations may

---

[1] " There has, therefore, grown up a rough general understanding that short-time paper is an unsuitable means of raising money for things like new equipment, from which the turnover is necessarily slow ; it should be used only to finance expenditure on materials and labour employed in making commodities that are likely to be sold before the maturity of the paper." (Pigou, *The Economics of Welfare,* p. 160.)

influence the expansion of credit by reason of the collateral status of securities in relation to both short and long term borrowing.[1]

By now it may be thought we have said enough to justify an inquiry into the accounting measurement of profit and we should wish to close this introduction to our subject by making some comment on the double entry technique employed by accountants in setting the day to day records and periodical summary statements of business enterprise. Since the time of its conscious innovation with the rise of medieval commerce [2] it has been clear to those most intimately concerned with the keeping of accounts that the method of double entry carries with it a vital statistical check in the sense that each recorded originating transaction has its reciprocal counterpart somewhere in the institutional system. Thus we see that when this system is extended on to the plane of a social economy an item of income in one context becomes an item of expenditure in another, and so on. By so disposing accounting classifications we are able to achieve a clear view of the mutual interdependence of otherwise economically distinct groups of transactions, and to so set the picture of events that we are assisted to right interpretations of historically recorded results.

---

[1] " In recent times, partly in consequence of the supersession of partnerships by joint stock companies, the proportion of national wealth represented by stocks and shares, and therefore, available as collateral security, has enormously increased." (Pigou, *The Economics of Welfare*, p. 164.)

[2] Dr. Peragallo adduces that " the most ancient double-entry books known to exist are those of the Massari of the Commune of Genoa, dating from the year 1340. These books are written in perfect double-entry form, which indicates that the system must have been in general use many years before." (*Origin and Evolution of Double Entry Bookkeeping. A Study of Italian Practice from the Fourteenth Century*, by Edward Peragallo, p. 3, New York, American Institute Publishing Company, 1938.)

II

THE NATURE OF INCOME AND CAPITAL [1]

IF we say that accounting is neither more nor less precise than most other skilled techniques which have discovered and served their purposes as practical aids to mankind in the ordinary business of life, we must also add that it lacks the discipline of definition. We start with an initial disadvantage as soon as we are brought face to face with an inquiry into the nature of two of its key terms. Income and capital are words common enough in everyday language, but no one would deny to them different meanings in different contexts. So it is with their use in accounting terminology, and much will depend upon whether we view them in a broad and descriptive sense or in a narrow and analytical sense. We shall begin by taking our inquiry into the former view.

The first duty of technical accounting is the plain recording of originating data in terms of the units of money associated with the incomings and outgoings of productive and, in a restricted connotation, institutional enterprises, financial intermediaries, insurance and social security agencies, public collective providers, and sometimes, for some purposes, final consumers. These originating transactions are perforce the subject of a preliminary sorting as between those which carry significance in relation to a time period intentionally set for comparatively short review, and those which are relatively less immediate in the sense of either internal durability conceived by the quality of delayed and gradual movement into the flow of the current, or exclusion by reason of external qualities of independence. This preliminary sorting of transactions broadly corresponds to a primary descriptive accounting differentiation between those items which relate to current account and those which relate to capital account, as commonly understood by economists ; those which are destined to find their place in the income or profit and loss account, and those which find relative stability in the balance sheet statement of assets, liabilities and proprietorship worth, as commonly understood by accountants. Within this compass of generic classification, in which the element of time plays so great a part, and conceptions of immediacy and reservation are the primary tests by which to reveal the secular intention of economic dealing, we are tempted to think of other words on which to fasten our meanings, and lest it should be thought that we favour

[1] First published in *Accounting Research*, Vol. 1, No. 1, November, 1948. (Cambridge University Press.)

revenue in place of income, we wish to make it clear that this does little to resolve the confusion, for in most contexts revenue and income are synonymous terms. In our view, current and resting are the better figures if the more particular connotations of the terms income and capital in general accounting usage are to be kept free from latent ambiguities.

Economists have always been quick to recognise this temporal qualification to economic transaction, and Professor Pigou has one passage in his *The Economics of Welfare* which does much to illuminate the conception of reservation which we have attached to the term resting. He says that

" For the present purpose [1] the precise content of capital is immaterial. However we define it, it may be likened to a lake into which a great variety of things, which are the fruit of savings, are continually being projected. These things, having once entered the lake, survive there for various periods, according to their several natures and the fortunes that befall them. Among them are things of long life, like elaborately built factories, things of moderate life, like machinery, and things of very short life, like material designed to be worked up into finished goods for consumption or coal destined to be burned. Length of life in this connection means, of course, length of life *as capital* in the industrial machine functioning as a going concern, not the length of life which a thing would enjoy if nobody interfered with it. Coal, for example, if left alone, will last without change of form for an indefinite number of years ; but, none the less, the ' life ' enjoyed by coal in the lake of capital, i.e. the period covered between its entrance and its exit, is almost always very short. All things that enter the lake eventually pass out of it again. Some of them pass, so to speak, in their own persons, embodied as material in some finished product, as when cotton yarn emerges as a cloth garment. But exits are not always, or indeed generally, made in the form of a passage outward of the actual elements that originally came in. When coal is burnt in the process of smelting iron, which is to be used eventually in making cutlery, it is the cutlery, embodying the ' virtue ' of the coal, and not the coal itself, which passes in person out of the lake. In like manner it is, of course, the ' virtue ' of machines that are worn out in making finished goods, and not the machines themselves, which passes out in person. In one form or another, however, whatever enters also leaves. There is then of necessity always a stream flowing out of the lake so long as it has any contents at all, and in practice there is also always a stream flowing into it. Its contents at any moment consist of everything that has flowed into it in the past *minus* anything that has flowed out. It is theoretically possible to make an inventory of them and also to evaluate them from day to day. When we speak, in connection with our definition of the national dividend, of the need for ' maintaining capital intact,' *something* is implied about the relation

---

[1] " What is meant by maintaining capital intact."

between successive inventories or successive evaluations of the contents of the lake we have been describing ".[1]

When reading this passage, accountants will not pass unnoticed the pointed references to " things of very short life, like material designed to be worked up into finished goods for consumption," or to those things which pass out " embodied as material in some finished product, as when cotton yarn emerges as a cloth garment." These are things which by operational intent change their nature and flow with such a degree of immediacy, as to carry high significance within a time period designedly set for comparatively short review. Such a feature sets them down as coming within the flow of the current. In the graphic phrasing of Professors Paton and Littleton, they are " goods or services which are highly transient in character and require assignment to revenue on the heels of acquisition ".[2]

The term resting has an odd sound in English accounting ears, and it may be well to add a more specific comment upon its use. It is a word of frequent occurrence in Central European accounting studies,[3] where it comes in to denote economic transactions of relatively static order lying outside dynamically conceived operating or profit and loss accounts. The near equivalent in English usage is capital account in the sense implied by economists, or again in the sense in which it turns up in a number of case law decisions bearing upon the profit distributions of joint stock companies. But in the accounting sense such a use of capital account is unsatisfactory, for as it stands it is equally capable of particular association with a specific kind of incoming (positive or negative) and of generic association with a variety of both incomings and outgoings not immediately taken into the flow of current operations. If we reserve its use to the former and particular association, clarity requires that we substitute another expression for the latter and generic association. The term resting is clear of this ambiguity, and seems appropriate to our purpose.

So far we have largely discussed the influence of time on the accounting distinction between current and resting transactions, and theoretically we have partially resolved our classification by finding an element of reservation in the latter class, making for delayed and gradual movement into the flow of the current, and by the assignment of relative immediacy to the items falling within the former class. But we have also made a passing reference to external qualities of independence as claiming attachment to some transactions of a resting

[1] *The Economics of Welfare*, by A. C. Pigou, Fourth Edition, pp. 43–44 (Macmillan, 1946).

[2] *An Introduction to Corporate Accounting Standards*, by W. A. Paton and A. C. Littleton, American Accounting Association, Monograph No. 3, 1940.

[3] Cf. the use of the word in Dr. Singer's *Standardised Accountancy in Germany* (Cambridge at the University Press, 1943).

12

order. Independence in this connection is related to the internal operating structure of particular enterprises, and is meant to imply external financial characteristics. Examples of this type of transaction are to be found in such incomings as are constituted by proprietorship contributions, external borrowing, items in the nature of redemptions and repayments, and in such outgoings as may represent subscriptions to new issues, the investment purchase of existing securities, and items for the redemption and repayment of obligations.

The dividing line between current and resting transactions is not so clear as might be commonly supposed, and we may have occasion to look at some of the more marginal cases when we come to deal with movements into the flow of the current, particularly those which are inherent in the common form of resting transaction represented by asset formation and deferred charge. But, as we might expect, it is the preliminary sorting of *outgoings* which can create perplexity when a precise attempt is made to set the line of demarcation. To meet this situation, accountants have directly associated capital expenditure, as they have called it, with resting outgoings made for the purpose of acquiring relatively durable or fixed assets [1] intended to be operationally employed in the course of business enterprise, and with constitutional outgoings such as the preliminary and formation expenses incidental to joint stock companies. Other outgoings falling within the category of deferred charges not directly intended to assert an influence on current operations, but which are expected to yield future benefits, such as certain kinds of advertising, are taken into the same generic classification. Current expenditure, on the other hand, is regarded as any form of outgoing associated with materials, labour and services, which benefits the immediate economic activity of a business, and which finds a place under one or other of the profit and loss groupings for production expenses, selling and distribution expenses, administration and management expenses, and so on.

In this rather more restricted usage, a resting outgoing amounts to little more than a transfer from circulating to relatively fixed resources. Nevertheless, it is not always so easy to decide if an outgoing associated with fixed assets is necessarily a resting item, and one of the tests commonly sought by accountants lies in the answer to the question whether or not the particular outgoing has done anything to *increase the life* of the asset with which it is related, or to promote an increase in its *efficiency* as measured either by output capacity and/or improved

---

[1] The Institute of Chartered Accountants, in its Recommendations on Accounting Principles, makes the point that " Fixed Assets, whatever be their nature or the type of business in which they are employed, have the fundamental characteristic that they are held with the object of earning revenue and not for the purpose of sale in the ordinary course of business." (IX. Depreciation of Fixed Assets, p. 24 (i)—Gee and Company (Publishers) Ltd.)

product quality. If the outgoing has merely kept up the asset by maintaining its effectiveness in the sense of *working* order, then it is regarded as a current cost. Thus, it comes about that accountants treat expenditures on additions to and extensions of fixed equipment as capital within the meaning of resting outgoings. Expenditures resulting in elements of improvement or betterment to existing assets are considered in much the same light if it can be substantiated that they do in fact promote increased efficiency. On the other hand, as we have seen, mundane expenditures on asset maintenance, repairs, the replacement of parts, and such like incidents to operational running, are ordinarily regarded as current outgoings.

Throughout this discussion we have sought to emphasise the importance of identifying the generic distinction between capital and current with those *actual* transactions, measurable in terms of units of money, which are promoted by the economic traversal of an enterprise along the paths of temporal periods intentionally limited for the purpose of recurrent survey, and in so doing we have commended a substitution of the adjectival use of the word capital by the term resting. This has brought us to the borders of such vital short term portrayals of institutional dispositions of resources as are conceived by economists to reside within their connotation of capital accounts, and accountants should sense it as strange that no such equivalent form directly accompanies the financial accounting documents prepared under the Single Account system, and which so far have been thought appropriate to reveal the state of a firm's affairs. The accounting statement of profit and loss is virtually an income account which takes in all the current transactions of an enterprise for a selected period of account. Thus it constitutes a statement of current flows, while the balance sheet purports a statement of the formula—assets minus liabilities equals proprietorship worth—at the close of an accounting period, and apart altogether from questions which concern its blatant mixture of historical and current costs, face values and arithmetical estimates, there is nowhere a plain statement illustrating those incomings and outgoings on resting or capital account which have taken place during the time interval marked by an accounting period. We suggest that the time has come for this anomaly to be remedied.

It is not difficult to set a technical form of resting account. On the one side will be found the straightforward incomings for new money capital contributions, new long term borrowing, and any redemptions and repayments associated with past lending activities. On the other side, direct outgoings will appear in respect of fixed asset formation, new lending in the shape of security investment, and any money outlays relating to the redemption and repayment of outstanding obligations constituted by past borrowing. Into this account will be credited business saving under the guise of retained profit, and those

14

items which make for a short conservation of circulating resources, such as provisions for depreciation and obsolescence, and changes in deferred taxation liabilities. Exceptional receipts (of a capital order), such as property insurance claims, will find their way to the credit of the resting account, whilst movements in deferred expenditure with the temporary character of asset formation will be disclosed among the debits in the same account. A special feature of the account is the balancing item established by the increase or decrease in circulating resources which should be analysed in terms of inventories, debtor and creditor claims, and money balances.[1]

We pass to the narrow view in which accountants have sought to attach rather more precise meanings to their use of the terms capital and income. If, for the moment, we set on one side the complications introduced by the conduct of business enterprise within the framework of statutory incorporation, we may regard capital in the strict accounting sense as equivalent to proprietorship worth. It is established by recording the amount of money or the money value of net assets made available to start an enterprise as moderated by later contributions and withdrawals, capital gains or losses, and by retained profits or losses on current account. For the substructure of this work the critical modification to recorded capital is so much of the reported profit on current account as is retained with the intention of adding to the store of wealth employed in the enterprise, or in the case of the less fortunate business the amount of the recorded loss which perforce encroaches upon that store of employed wealth. Our use of the phrase " store of employed wealth " is open to serious challenge in the sense in which we have slipped it into the preceding passage, but if we seem to fall into a wilful ambiguity we do so, not waywardly but designedly, with the intent of drawing attention to a vital distinction between the narrow accounting concept of capital and the economic ideas served by the use of the same term. For the economist, capital " consists of all those goods, existing at a particular time, which can be used in any way so as to satisfy wants during the subsequent period ".[2] It is composed of a stock of wealth in the sense of material things or their equivalent—tangible assets, and although for some purposes such an intangible possessional attribute as goodwill may find a separate place in value summations of wealth, it can never exist apart from either the tangible assets of which it is the expression of effective organisation, or the acquired skill associated with the work of professionally escorted ventures.

---

[1] A form of Resting Account which may be readily adapted to the circumstances and requirements of individual firms is set out in section vii of the writer's *Social Accounts and the Business Enterprise Sector of the National Economy*, shortly to be published by the Cambridge University Press.

[2] J. R. Hicks, *The Social Framework*, p. 73 (Oxford, 1942).

In the practical conduct of business affairs accountants are expected to limit their perspective to the subject of domestic entities, and within this compass they have been trained to record and survey quantifiably measurable economic transactions from a twofold or double standpoint. It therefore comes about that elementally the amount of money or money's worth coming in to start an enterprise is looked upon as the originating capital to be separately identified from the fixed and circulating assets acquired by payment outgoing or agreed valuation. For all accounting purposes this distinction is precise, and there is always a clear line of demarcation between the fund of money capital contributed to an enterprise or saved by its proprietors, and the general pool of assets acquired and organised for the achievement of the objects of that enterprise, to which such fund lays claim. Thus it comes about that the nature of capital in accounting usage is commonly to be discerned on the former façade of this twofold statement, and in this strict and particular view it is invariably recorded proprietorship worth which comes to the fore when accountants are confronted with the term capital. It would not seem too chimerical to see in this double standpoint a first cause of much that is perplexing in conventional accounting when viewed in the light of its close attachment to historical costs. The originating fixed assets of a business are more often than not acquired out of the money capital introduced into that business by its proprietors. Even when they are not so directly acquired, there is usually a presumption that they were taken over at a money valuation which formed the basis for a record of originating proprietorship worth. In the technique of accounting there is always a strong tie between proprietorship worth and the assets to which it lays claim, and so it comes about that the primary record of a purchased fixed asset in the books of an enterprise is always made at the amount of money for which it was bought. This is not to say that occasions do not arise when assets are revalued for the purpose of accounting record, but it does mean that whenever that happens a counterbalancing adjustment is always necessary to the monetary statement of proprietorship worth. Before we leave some of the questions which are implicit in this discussion, we should take this opportunity to point out that, apart altogether from matters which concern the protection of contributed money capital, it is important to recognise that nearly all existing accounting conventions are valid in what economists call a stationary state. We shall have more to say on this subject in a later chapter, particularly when we come to deal with the accounting transfers from asset formation to operating expenditure in circumstances which rely upon a tacit assumption of price level stability.

The association of asset formation with contributed money capital is peculiarly emphasised in the case of such public utility undertakings as are required to present their published accounts in the form delineated by accountants as the Double Account system. Indeed, it is the primary object of this method of presentation to show on the one hand the money capital subscribed[1] for the purposes of the undertaking, and on the other hand the extent of its application in asset formation. Social opinion, endorsed by the force of law, has regarded such disclosure as essential not only by reason of the public nature of railway, gas, electricity, water and such-like companies, but because the construction and working of these undertakings involves high original capital outlays which must be kept up. As a technical matter, such disclosure is achieved by presenting a balance sheet which is divided into two sections. The first section is constituted in the form of a straightforward debit and credit account which on the one side sets out appropriate details of money capital receipts and on the other side classified expenditure on asset formation. The appearance of this part of the balance sheet is uncommonly like the type of account which economists would presumably designate as capital, though it must be admitted that such a Double Accounting design has been promoted rather more by legal constraint than by economic concept. The balance, or in some cases the totals, of this first sectional account is carried to a statement set out in the common form of balance sheet as ordinarily prepared under the Single Account system, where it is brought into relation with the circulating capital resources of the undertaking. As a commentary on the Double Account system, it may be remarked that in its original conception it was not intended that depreciation should be provided by proportionate allocations to operating accounts of original costs of fixed assets, as obtained, and still obtains, under the Single Account system. As a corollary to the maintenance of original capital outlay, the principle sought was that of charging to operating account all repairs, renewals and replacements as and when they were made. Economically there was much to be said for this intention, so long as heavy and disproportionate renewals were not congested in any one period. In most cases, apprehension of this possibility has led to the raising of depreciation and renewal funds designed to spread charges of this order over the accounting periods served by the employment of fixed assets.

In the early part of this discussion we noticed the meanings which economists ascribe to their use of the expressions capital and current accounts, and we have been concerned to examine the affinity of this prospect with the concepts of accounting terminology. Accordingly, we think it well to remark on one particular use of these expressions which might mislead those who are not trained accountants. Thus, accountants are accustomed to a proprietorship distinction between

[1] In this public utility context money capital receipts are usually taken to include debentures and loans.

17

capital and current [1] in the accounts of partnership ventures, although for balance sheet purposes both lie within the classification of proprietorship worth. To make the matter clear, a partner's capital account simply records the amount of money, in the restricted accounting sense of the term capital, which he has directly subscribed, or is regarded as having contributed, to a partnership venture, and which is usually determined by the constraint of a partnership agreement. A partner's current account ordinarily records the amount of partnership profits appropriated to his share and the withdrawals which require to be set against it. An undrawn balance represents profits retained and utilised for the purposes of the partnership ; it constitutes the current claim of a particular partner on the assets of the firm. Similarly, an overdrawn balance denotes the current claim of the firm on the private assets of a particular partner, and in some agreements these factors are acknowledged by the inclusion of an article which provides for interest on current account balances to be given due recognition in the accounts of the firm.

In our attempt to explain the accounting use of the term capital we have so far thought of it in relation to business enterprises for the very natural reason that accountants are most intimately concerned with the affairs of the business world. Although they are frequently called upon to measure the taxable income of *private individuals*, they are rather less frequently, though by no means uncommonly, asked to measure money capital. Thus it comes about that in accounting usage the term capital—apart from its somewhat special technical connection with the affairs of deceased estates, executorship and settlement trusts—is not so often applied to the personal affairs of individuals. On occasions the accountant is asked to prepare a statement of the assets and liabilities of a private individual, but this is rather more particularly the case where that individual is in possession of substantial property assets and/or security investments. If pressed to assign a meaning to the general notion of an individual's capital, most accountants would probably think in terms of the money value of the assets to which he has title in his private capacity, imputed in accordance with such conventions as are commonly applied to business accounts, less the monetary notation of all forms of creditor claims for which he is personally responsible. Thus the accountant would arrive at the ascription of a money value to personal net assets from a standpoint which virtually regards the affairs of a private individual in much the same light as those of an enterprise. At any one time these assets would include a person's durable goods, his properties,

[1] Another technical accounting use of the qualifying word " current " is that which applies it to the running, reciprocal and pivotal accounts between holding, subsidiary and associated companies, and between the head office and branches of a large-scale business.

his security investments, the accounting capital which he employs in his own business, his share of the accounting capital employed in any firm of which he is a partner, his bank and cash balances, and in strict theory an inventory of such consumable goods as he has on hand. As one might expect, there is a similarity between this statement of an individual's capital and the make up of a deceased person's estate as required to be disclosed for death duty purposes. Thus, an Inland Revenue Affidavit which sets out the details of the estate at the date of death follows the order of security investments, cash in the house, bank balances, mortgages, bills and promissory notes, debts, life insurance policies, household goods and personal effects, stock in trade, goodwill of business, a partnership share, leasehold properties and reversionary interests. From this personal property a deduction is made for debts and expenses, and an addition for the net value of real property (i.e. after providing for any incumbrances).[1] It will be noticed, in theory at any rate, that accountants would treat durable goods as residing within the province of an individual's capital in the sense normally ascribed to fixed assets. As a matter of statistical convenience, it is not usual to so distinguish durable use goods in the ordinary run of applied economic investigations, and with the exception of the particular assets comprised by land and buildings it is usual to treat such goods as falling within the connotation of current consumption. Nevertheless, we cannot overlook the fact that when accountants are called upon to prepare the private accounts of individuals, their instructions are not infrequently limited to a review of investments in the sense of properties and securities.

It will also be noticed that within the terms so far thought relevant to the discussion in this chapter we have dropped into use the expression " capital employed." It may be doubted whether the conception of capital employed necessarily adds anything to the accounting notion of proprietorship worth, for it means very much the same thing, with the possible exception that long term borrowed money may, on occasion, fall to be regarded as a claimant for inclusion in the former though it certainly would not find a place in the latter classification. The expression " capital employed " is one of comparatively recent innovation in the language of accounts, and it seems to have come into greater prominence during the war not only by reason of taxation legislation designed to remove excess profits, but also in relation to the profit element in certain government contracts which in some instances was regarded as having something to do with the ratio of employed capital to cost of turnover, following the assumption of a reasonable standard percentage for return on capital. It is probable that a strict accounting view of employed capital would limit it to

[1] Cf. The Form of Executorship Accounts in *Design of Accounts* (Oxford University Press, 1944) pp. 171–172.

contributed money capital plus accumulated savings in whatever forms they might be classified in balance sheets.

We turn to those matters of impersonal ownership which lend qualifications to capital as a term of account connected with the constitutional structures of corporate enterprises. If we chance to look at a published company balance sheet, it is probable that one of the first items to catch our eyes will be the authorised or, as it is sometimes called, nominal capital. As the qualifying adjective implies, this is the amount of money capital which a corporate body is authorised by its constitution to raise for the purposes of its undertaking, without recourse to a legal process necessarily related to any increase beyond that originally contemplated on formation. It is not an intrinsic entry in the recorded accounts, and is therefore looked upon as an inset note to the balance sheet which company legislation requires. It may or may not be wholly subscribed, but such part as is subscribed, and which commonly passes under the title of issued capital, constitutes at least part of the money which so far has been put into, or deemed to have been contributed to, a corporate body (ordinarily a joint stock company) by its proprietorship members, and as such it takes pride of place among the primary entries recorded in the accounts. Nevertheless, it would be a mistake to imagine that the issued capital of a company represents *all* the money which has been paid in by the proprietorship members. The issue of stocks and shares at a premium above their nominal equivalents is a normal experience of the modern investment capital market, and it is quite clear that the amount of the premium is none the less contributed money. What, then, is the reason for the distinction denominated to issued capital? This is a point which has been well taken by Professors Paton and Littleton. Their statement of the matter, as seen from the American standpoint, is couched in the following terms. " It must be recognised that the corporation is a business enterprise as well as a legal entity. This duality requires of accounting the difficult task of presenting economic data as well as reflecting the purely legal aspect. The difficulty is perhaps most marked in connection with the reporting of capital, for here business and legal concepts are quite different. In law there is a tendency to view capital as a designated quantity which sets a limit upon the withdrawal of funds invested by the stockholders. (The term is also used more broadly in business to suggest the total equity of the stockholders at a particular point or the total of all resources in use in the enterprise regardless of source.) Business needs are not adequately served if the terminology and organisation of the statements are too strongly influenced by legal concepts and considerations ".[1] The legal position is not dissimilar

[1] *An Introduction to Corporate Accounting Standards*, by W. A. Paton and A. C. Littleton, p. 106 (American Accounting Association, 1940).

20

in this country, and the money contributions of the proprietorship members of a corporate enterprise which are taken within the designation of issued capital are legally thought of as resilient to setbacks which otherwise might encroach upon the claims of creditors. It is for this reason that legal constraints are imposed upon the return or reduction of issued capital. The legal situation was made quite plain in the case of Guinness *v.* Land Corporation of Ireland, and the relevant part of the judgment in that case enunciated the principle that " ... the capital of the company as mentioned in the Memorandum is to be the fund which is to pay the creditors in the event of the company being wound up. From that it follows that whatever has been paid by a member cannot be returned to him. In my opinion, it also follows that what is described in the Memorandum as capital, cannot be diverted from the objects of the society. It is, of course, liable to be spent or lost in carrying on the business of the company, but no part of it can be returned to a member so as to take away from the fund to which the creditors have a right to look, as that out of which they are to be paid ".[1]

It is interesting to observe the legal situation in regard to those money contributions of proprietorship members which take the form of share premiums. It seems that unless there were explicit prohibiting provisions in a company's articles of association, there was nothing in the Companies Acts, up to and including 1929, which hindered the application of such premiums as capital gains distributable as income. No one could claim that such a course was sound, for clearly it would place share premiums in the same category as distributable profits so far as concerned availability for dividend. Thus, as Mr. de Paula has pointed out, if a dividend was paid out of share premiums it would amount to a return to the shareholders of amounts which they themselves had subscribed.[2] This anomaly was recognised by the Cohen Committee on Company Law Amendment, which reported to Parliament in June, 1945. Paragraph 108 of that report said quite firmly that " share premiums are in essence capital though the assets acquired therewith do not represent the capital account strictly so called and there is no legal object, apart from any provision in the articles, to prevent the distribution thereof by way of dividend. In our view this is undesirable." Appropriately enough, therefore, it was recommended " that a Section be added to the Act providing that as from the coming into force of the new Act, the provisions of the Companies Act, 1929, relating to the reduction of share capital shall apply to any premiums received on the issue of shares of the company (whether received before or after the coming into force of the new

[1] (1883) 22 Ch. D. 349.

[2] Cf. *The Principles of Auditing*, by F. R. M. de Paula, pp. 186–187 (Pitman, Tenth Edition).

21

Act) as if the share premium account were paid-up share capital save so far as lawfully applied for other purposes before the coming into force of the new Act." Quite properly, it was also provided that notwithstanding this contemplated section " such premiums may be applied by the company in or towards paying up unissued shares of the company to be issued to the members of the company ".[1] It will be seen that the purpose of these recommendations was to place the money contributions of proprietorship members represented by issued capital, and share premiums, on much the same footing, and Section 72 of the Companies Act, 1947, has now given to these recommendations the force of statutory authority. It is worth noting, however, that sub-section (3) of the said Section 72 still allows a share premium account to be applied in writing off—" (a) the preliminary expenses of the company ; or (b) the expenses of, or the commission paid or discount allowed on, any issue of shares or debentures of the company ; or in providing for the premium payable on redemption of any redeemable preference shares or of any debentures of the company."[2] Since share premiums are now to be regarded on much the same plane as issued capital in relation to the return or reduction of share capital in a company, it follows that such premiums may serve as an additional buffer for the protection of creditors, and the legal compulsion to maintain issued money capital intact is virtually extended to the premiums, so that henceforth accounting technique will look essentially to the preservation of the money subscribed, or deemed to have been contributed to a company by its members.

Money capital may be subscribed and issued in the form of particular types of shares or stocks. These types are largely distinguishable by the terms and conditions under which they are issued, considerations so designed as to safeguard the attraction of money into the enterprise in a manner consistent with the particular circumstances current at the time of monetary capital requirement. It will be recognised that these types may be varied according to the stability of the particular enterprise, the objects for which it was formed, and the conditions of the money capital investment market at the time of issue. In general, it will be found that money capital is issued in one or other of two broad categories, customarily denoted as preference and ordinary. As we have indicated, there are a number of refinements within these comprehensive classifications, but as a general rule we may take it that preference shares or stocks are entitled to a fixed dividend out of distributable profits, while ordinary shares or stocks lay claim to the balance, a balance of profits which may or may not be withdrawn according to the financial necessities of the undertaking. It is left to

[1] *Report of the Committee on Company Law Amendment*, Cmd. 6659, p. 64 (London, His Majesty's Stationery Office, June, 1945).

[2] Now Section 56, Companies Act, 1948.

the articles of association to determine whether or not the preferred money capital has a preferential claim on the assets of the corporation in the event of liquidation, but it is a well established principle of English company law that if the articles do not so provide then the preference and ordinary share or stock holders are evenly matched so far as concerns the return of money capital on liquidation. The preferred right to a fixed dividend may be either cumulative or non-cumulative. If it is cumulative, then in the event of an insufficiency of annual distributable profits it carries the right to recover arrears in later years, if then the profits are adequate to such declared withdrawals. This cumulative right sets an embargo upon the payment of dividends to ordinary shareholders, for they cannot receive anything until all the preference arrears have been honoured by declaration and payment. If the right to a fixed dividend is non-cumulative, the preference shareholders are only so entitled out of the distributable profits of each year, and there is no power to recover arrears out of the profits of later years. It should be explained that in England there is a presumption that all preference shares carry cumulative dividend rights unless the company's articles expressly provide that they shall be non-cumulative. There are some cases in which the articles empower the preference shares to participate in surplus distributable profits remaining after payment of their own fixed dividend *and* a specified rate of dividend on the ordinary shares ; when such provisions attach the shares are known as participating preference shares.

Ordinary shares or stocks find their place within that class of security investments known as equities. As will be recognised from the preceding discussion, an equity security is one which carries rights to the residuary net assets and profits of a body corporate after the money capital and fixed interest claims of securities with preferred rights have been taken into account. In times of rising prices there is a tendency to the investment of money in equity securities, and there is usually some relaxation of pressure on fixed interest securities. The reasons ordinarily adduced in evidence of this course of action imply a change of security emphasis, for security of repayment of money capital, coupled with a fixed rate of interest, is then of less consequence than security of real value sought in those underlying assets of the enterprise which are not constituted by monetary claims. Thus, it is felt that rights to residuary net assets and profits present lesser risks in inflationary periods. Later in this work we shall have occasion to reconsider the questions raised by these apprehensions.

As is well known to accountants, the Companies Act of 1929 permitted the issue of shares at a discount provided they were *of a class already issued*. At the time when this Act came into force, such legal sanction was a relatively new departure from the previous standpoint of English company law, a standpoint which was, and still is, very much concerned to preserve the integrity of *contributed money* capital. Accordingly, this sanction was hedged around with strict conditions and no relaxing changes were made in the general amending legislation of 1947. Thus, the issue of the shares at a discount must be authorised by resolution passed in general meeting of the company, and must be sanctioned by the court. The resolution must specify the maximum rate of discount at which the shares are to be issued, and at the date of the issue not less than one year must have elapsed since the date on which the company was entitled to commence business.[1] As we have noticed, the issue of shares at a discount is not a matter which is entirely within the competence of the company, for it is specifically provided that " where a company has passed a resolution authorising the issue of shares at a discount, it may apply to the court for an order sanctioning the issue, and on any such application the court, if, having regard to all the circumstances of the case, it thinks proper so to do, may make an order sanctioning the issue on such terms and conditions as it thinks fit ".[2] Moreover, the shares which are to be issued at a discount must be so issued within one month after the date on which the court gives its sanction, or within such extended time as the court may allow.[3] Thus in those cases where there has been an abandonment of the principle that shares are liable to be fully paid for, the court asserts its supervision, and the law requires that the crux of the matter shall be made plain to the public, by providing that " every prospectus relating to the issue of the shares and every balance sheet issued by the company subsequently to the issue of the shares must contain particulars of the discount allowed on the issue of the shares or of so much of that discount as has not been written off at the date of the issue of the document in question ".[4]

English accounting practice, following the statutory requirement to which we have referred, is accustomed to the portrayal of the appropriate stated issued capital at its full face money value, as though it was deemed to have been contributed as such, thereby treating the amount of the discount on the issue as being in the nature of deferred expenditure the benefit of which will inure in the future. This interpretation gives heed to the discount as an item calling for inclusion among the assets in the balance sheet, until such time as it is written off by charges, relevant to the cause of the

---

[1] Companies Act, 1929, Section 47 (1) (*a*), (*b*) and (*c*) ; Section 57 (1) (*a*), (*b*) and (*c*), 1948 Act.

[2] 1929 Act, Section 47 (2) ; Section 57 (2), 1948 Act.

[3] 1929 Act, Section 47 (1) (*d*) ; Section 57 (1) (*d*), 1948 Act.

[4] 1929 Act, Section 47 (3) ; Section 57 (3) and Eighth Schedule 3 (*e*), 1948 Act.

24

expenditure, in the non-operating section of subsequent profit and loss accounts. American accounting practice, on the other hand, is still anxious to identify the total amount of money actually subscribed by the proprietorship members for the purposes of the enterprise, and it does not show itself quite so concerned to emphasise the final nominal amount which may be due to the stock or share holders, though it must not be inferred that it neglects this point. Thus, two prominent American academic accountants, whom we have already had occasion to mention, have asserted that " no form of recording or presentation which permits the amount of true capital investment to be obscured is in harmony with fundamental concepts and standards. If stock has a formal par or stated value it is not improper to show such a figure in the balance sheet, but care must be taken to attach thereto the amount of any premium or paid-in ' surplus,' or deduct the amount of any discount or overvaluation, so that the total amount paid in by the stockholder is displayed in clear cut fashion ".[1]

It seems well to mention that English company law permits the issue of redeemable preference shares, but in due conformity with its inclination to preserve money capital intact it provides that on redemption, otherwise than out of the proceeds of a fresh issue, a sum shall be transferred to a capital redemption reserve fund, out of profits otherwise available for dividend, equivalent to the nominal amount of the shares so redeemed.[2] Moreover, any premium which may be payable on redemption is to be provided for out of the profits of the company not only where the shares are redeemed out of the proceeds of a fresh issue, but in all cases save for the one rather odd alternative which permits a company's share premium account to be so utilised.[3] Hence it is not difficult to see the legislative store which is placed on safeguarding the integrity of the money capital actually paid into a company for the purpose of carrying out its objects. In this context there are other statutory provisions which should not pass unnoticed. Thus authority for the issue of redeemable preference shares must be contained in the company's articles of association and the shares which are to be redeemable must be so issued in that form. It is not open to the company to resolve that they shall be redeemable *after* the shares have been issued. Again, the shares must be fully paid up before they can be redeemed, and the actual redemption is not to be taken as reducing the amount of the authorised share capital. There is the usual requirement of accounting disclosure, which in this case provides for the inclusion of a statement in every balance

---

[1] *An Introduction to Corporate Accounting Standards*, by W. A. Paton and A. C. Littleton, p. 41 (American Accounting Association, 1940).

[2] Section 71, Companies Act, 1947 ; Section 58, 1948 Act.

[3] Sections 71 and 72, Companies Act, 1947 ; Section 58, 1948 Act.

sheet of a company which has issued redeemable preference shares specifying what part of the issued capital of the company consists of such shares, and the earliest date on which the company has power to redeem the shares. It should be remarked that where a company has redeemed or is about to redeem any preference shares, it has the power to issue shares up to the nominal amount of the shares redeemed or to be redeemed as if those shares had never been issued. We should add that the capital redemption reserve fund created by transfer out of profits otherwise available for dividend is treated in the same way as paid-up capital, and it is expressly indicated that the statutory provisions relating to the reduction of the share capital of a company with the sanction of the court shall apply to the capital redemption reserve fund. Thus it is quite clear that this particular reserve fund is not available for the payment of dividends, though it may be applied in paying up unissued shares of the company to be issued as bonus shares.[1]

Modern English accounting usage favours a balance sheet disposition of proprietorship worth in terms of two major categories designated as (1) contributed money capital and capital reserves, and (2) revenue reserves and surplus. In the balance sheet of an English company the first category would be resolved by the following entries :—

1. Issued Capital suitably summarised to indicate the different types of shares or stocks ;
2. Capital Redemption Reserve Fund ;
3. Premium Accounts ;
4. Capital Reserves.

Entries one, two and three we have already explained. Entry four, described as capital reserves, received a measure of definition in the Report of the Cohen Committee on Company Law Amendment. At page 59 of that Report, capital reserves were defined as " any amounts which, whether or not they were originally set aside as provisions to meet any diminution in value of assets, specific liability, contingency or commitment known to exist as at the date of the balance sheet, are not retained for that purpose and are not regarded as free for distribution through the profit and loss, or income and expenditure account." At first sight this definition appears to be ambiguous, but it seems to have arisen out of the general stand taken by the Committee on the controversial subject of undisclosed reserves, and it is worth while looking at what the Committee had to say on this matter. At paragraph 101 of the Report, the whole question was treated in some detail, and in a manner which no reasonable person could possibly take exception to so far as concerns the ordinary run of companies. The three special classes of companies where special

---

[1] Section 46, Companies Act, 1929 ; Section 71, 1947 Act ; Section 58, 1948 Act.

stability considerations must be taken into account, namely, banking companies, discount companies, and assurance and insurance companies, were considered separately, with a view to granting special disclosure exemptions the reasons for which need not detain us here. On the more general approach the Committee pointed out that " the chief matter which has aroused controversy is the question of undisclosed or, as they are frequently called, secret or inner reserves. An undisclosed reserve is commonly created by using profits to write down more than is necessary such assets as investments, freehold and leasehold property or plant and machinery ; by creating excessive provisions for bad debts or other contingencies ; by charging capital expenditure to revenue ; or by under-valuing stock in trade. Normally the object of creating an undisclosed reserve is to enable a company to avoid violent fluctuations in its published profits or its dividends.

The objections urged against undisclosed reserves can be summarised as follows. As the assets are undervalued or the liabilities overstated, the balance sheet does not present a true picture of the state of the company's affairs ; the balance of profit disclosed as available for dividends is diminished, and the market value of the shares may accordingly be lower than it might otherwise be ; and the creation, existence or use of reserves, known only to the directors, may place them in an invidious position when buying or selling the shares.

On the other hand, if there is no detailed disclosure in the profit and loss account, undisclosed reserves accumulated in past periods may be used to swell the profits in years when the company is faring badly, and the shareholders may be misled into thinking that the company is making profits when such is not the case. Such abuses are rare, and, in general, directors have concealed reserves from shareholders in the belief that such concealment is in the interests of the company. None the less the practice has the unfortunate result that shareholders and investors and their advisers have not the information to enable them to estimate the real value of the shares.

We do not believe that, if fully informed, shareholders would press for excessive dividends, and we are in favour of as much disclosure as practicable. It is also important in our opinion to ensure that there should be adequate disclosure and publication of the results of companies so as to create confidence in the financial management of industry and to dissipate any suggestion that hidden profits are being accumulated by industrial concerns to the detriment of consumers and those who work for industry ".[1]

There we have the hub of the matter, which in some measure may be taken as explaining the entanglement of amounts originally set

[1] *The Report of the Committee on Company Law Amendment*, June, 1945, p. 56 (Cmd. 6659, London : His Majesty's Stationery Office).

aside as provisions to meet any diminution in value of assets, specific liability, contingency or commitment, but not retained for that purpose and not regarded as free for distribution, as included in the definition of capital reserves to which we have referred. Were it not for the Committee's justifiable preoccupation with non-disclosure, it would have been more simple to define capital reserves as amounts set aside, either out of capital gains or profits, which are not regarded as free for distribution through the profit and loss, or income and expenditure, account.

Mr. F. R. M. de Paula refers to capital reserves as those created out of surpluses of a capital nature, such as a surplus arising out of a revaluation of fixed assets, realised capital profits, profits prior to incorporation, and such-like items.[1]

Mr. S. W. Rowland defines a capital reserve quite baldly as one " derived from a source which precludes the possibility that it may be distributed as dividend ".[2] For ourselves we are content to regard capital reserves as being constituted by capital gains which are not intended to be applied as income, by economic replacement provisions in excess of those calculated by reference to original cost duly consummated as capital by actual asset replacements, and the all important economic reconciling consideration represented by any surplus on revaluation of assets or liabilities.[3]

To return to our English company balance sheet, the second category, designated as revenue reserves and surplus, would be attended by the following entries :—

1. Free Revenue Reserves ;
2. Profit and Loss Account Balance.

Again, it is instructive to look at the Report of the Cohen Committee on Company Law Amendment for a definition of free revenue reserves. There, at page 60, we find reserves other than capital reserves, presumably free revenue reserves, defined as " any amounts which, having been set aside out of revenue or other surpluses " and which " are free in that they are not retained to meet any diminution in value of assets, specific liability, contingency or commitment known to exist as at the date of the balance sheet." It is interesting to conjecture what is meant by the words " or other surpluses " in the above

[1] Cf. *The Principles of Auditing*, by F. R. M. de Paula, Tenth Edition, pp. 142 and 192 (London : Sir Isaac Pitman and Sons Ltd., 1945).

[2] *Accounting*, by Stanley W. Rowland, p. 246 (The Home University Library, Thornton Butterworth, 1936).

[3] Apart altogether from purely monetary changes, a positive adjustment conceived as a credit to Capital Reserve, and arising out of a periodical revaluation of net assets, might very well constitute a measure of the benefit accruing to an enterprise by reason of the effective organisation of its assets in production—goodwill, as accountants would call it.

definition, but presumably this would include capital gains intended and constitutionally permitted to be applied as income. In our view, free revenue reserves have their source in profits, and non-operating income, retained in the enterprise by exclusion from distribution and set aside as specific credits available for future use. They would include such items as general reserves set aside out of income " to provide against unknown future contingencies, to increase the working capital, to equalise dividends, or merely to strengthen the financial position of the concern," [1] and reserve and sinking funds similarly created out of income.

The profit and loss account balance is entirely free from any question of reservation or lesser immediacy, and may be utilised for distribution to proprietors as circumstances may require. Perhaps we may question the merit of creating free revenue reserves as something taken out of and regarded as apart from the general fund of undistributed profits, for it is seldom that there is any real distinction between the two, unless it be that the process of earmarking is felt to psychologically engender a spirit of restraint in regard to dividends and withdrawals. To some persons unfamiliar with such technical features of accounts, the distinction is puzzling, and even some accountants question its usefulness. Professors Paton and Littleton, writing from the American standpoint, put the matter thus.

" The classification of surplus in terms of the uses to which the expanded funds are put is largely hypothetical, but interpretative indications may be given from time to time to show the portions which by implication are embodied in working assets or fixed assets. All surplus may be viewed as a general purpose buffer or margin, and there is little to be gained by appropriating surplus under special titles to reflect possibility of loss or readiness to face contingencies."

In rather more detail these authors remark that " the earmarking of surplus as special reserves is likely to convey a misleading impression to the average reader of statements. The term ' reserve ' suggests to many people an actual fund of cash or similar resources which is being accumulated for a specific purpose. Actually there is usually no segregated fund matching the ' reserve ' and often there neither has been nor will be an investment or expenditure of funds of the nature implied by the name of the reserve." They go on to suggest that

" particularly questionable is the practice of appropriating surplus under special titles designed to reflect the possibility of loss and the readiness of the corporation to face the contingency. All surplus may be viewed as a general-purpose buffer or reserve, and there is little to be gained by the use of fancy labels in this connection. If claims exist which presumably must be satisfied the amount thereof, estimated if need be, should be set up as a liability. If the contingency

[1] *The Principles of Auditing*, op. cit., pp. 140–141.

is nothing more than a bare possibility, and especially if the amount of possible loss is indeterminate, a footnote is likely to be more informative than a subdividing of surplus. In no event should a reserve for possible future loss be reported in such a manner as to obscure its true character as a portion of surplus ".[1]

With these views we find ourselves in considerable sympathy, for quite clearly there is little or no fundamental difference between a free revenue reserve and a profit and loss account balance. Both items, as they stand in an English company balance sheet at the present time, represent earned business savings as measured in terms of historical costs and revenues, and the only possible validity for the distinction lies in executive decisions to distinguish the degrees in which it is intended that earnings are to be regarded as available for distribution to the shareholding proprietors. Fundamentally, the amount of accounting surplus over and above the money capital adventured into a business is made up of the sum of the retained profits of the past up to the beginning of the accounting period at the close of which the balance sheet is drawn, the retained profit of the current accounting period, and capital reserves in the sense in which we have already considered them duly summated from the beginning of the enterprise to the beginning of the current accounting period, and carrying in any additions or deductions of a similar order relevant to the current accounting period. Before we pass from this subject we should notice the Companies Act of 1947, which requires that " the aggregate amounts respectively of capital reserves, revenue reserves and provisions (other than provisions for depreciation, renewals or diminution in value of assets) shall be stated under separate headings." As a matter of disclosure we should also observe the paragraph which provides that—

" (1) There shall also be shown (unless it is shown in the profit and loss account or a statement or report annexed thereto, or the amount involved is not material)—

(*a*) where the amount of the capital reserves, of the revenue reserves or of the provisions (other than provisions for depreciation, renewals or diminution in value of assets) shows an increase as compared with the amount at the end of the immediately preceding financial year, the source from which the amount of the increase has been derived ; and

(*b*) where—

(i) the amount of the capital reserves or of the revenue reserves shows a decrease as compared with the amount at the end of the immediately preceding financial year ; or

[1] *An Introduction to Corporate Accounting Standards*, by W. A. Paton and A. C. Littleton, pp. 97, 108 and 109 (American Accounting Association, 1940).

(ii) the amount at the end of the immediately preceding financial year of the provisions (other than provisions for depreciation, renewals or diminution in value of assets) exceeded the aggregate of the sums since applied and amounts still retained for the purposes thereof;

· the application of the amounts derived from the difference.

(2) Where the heading showing any of the reserves or provisions aforesaid is divided into sub-headings, this paragraph shall apply to each of the separate amounts shown in the sub-headings instead of applying to the aggregate amount thereof".[1]

American accounting usage adopts somewhat similar classifications to those which we have enunciated in respect of English accounting usage, although it tends to call them by other names. Thus there are three fundamental categories usually described as stated or adventured capital, paid in and unearned surplus, and, lastly, earned surplus. Professor H. R. Hatfield makes the point that " stated capital, as an accounting term, represents so much of the stockholders' contribution as is understood to be an inviolable buffer to protect creditors, and possibly other stockholders, and ordinarily is not to be paid back to them." He asserts that surplus, as an accounting term, represents any excess of proprietorship over capital as so defined, and he requires that both capital and surplus should be kept distinct. He says quite clearly that a distinction should also be maintained between earned surplus and capital surplus, although in his opinion both are alike surplus.[2] In this context it is plain that capital surplus corresponds to what English accountants call capital reserves and premium accounts, while earned surplus is analogous to free revenue reserves and profit and loss balances.

There are other qualifying expressions which accountants have applied to capital, one of the most contradictory of which may be said to be the label " loan capital." In the ordinary way, loan capital is very largely long term borrowed money which is taken into or contributed to an enterprise mainly through the medium of a charge on the assets in the shape of a debenture. Sometimes we meet the terms " fixed and circulating capitals." In the light of the discussion in this chapter, these expressions are misleading in that they properly relate to assets. Historically they have arisen out of legal judgments

---

[1] Paragraphs 3 and 4, First Schedule—Accounts Part I., General Provisions as to Balance Sheet and Profit and Loss Account, A. Balance Sheet : Companies Act, 1947, Paragraphs 6 and 7, Eighth Schedule, 1948 Act.

[2] *Surplus and Dividends*, by Professor H. R. Hatfield, *Dickinson Lectures in Accounting*, p. 23 (Harvard University Press, 1943).

which have tended to regard assets and capital as synonymous terms.[1]

In accounting usage we frequently meet the expression " working capital." In the ordinary sense in which it is so used it implies the excess of current assets over current liabilities, and apart from the inclusion of inventories in the concept of working capital it very largely represents what economists would regard as monetary claims. In this connection it is interesting to observe that the report of the Cohen Committee on Company Law Amendment defined " current assets " as cash and assets held for conversion into cash (p. 58), while the Recommendations on Accounting Principles of the Institute of Chartered Accountants in England and Wales [2] sought to include in this group " such assets as are held for realisation in the ordinary course of business " and indicated that they would " normally include : (a) stock-in-trade and work-in-progress ; (b) trade and other debtors, prepayments and bills receivable ; (c) investments held as part of the liquid resources of the company ; (d) tax reserve certificates ; (e) bank balances and cash." A significant note was added to the effect that " Debts of material amount not due until after the lapse of one year from the date of the balance sheet should be separately grouped and suitably described," that is, they should be excluded from the grouping for current assets. The same publication regarded " Current Liabilities and Provisions " as " including, *inter alia*, (a) trade liabilities, bills payable and accrued charges ; (b) bank loans and overdrafts ; (c) other short-term loans ; (d) interest accrued on debentures and long-term liabilities ; (e) provision for current taxation ; (f) provisions to meet specific commitments or contingencies where the amounts involved cannot be determined with substantial accuracy ; and (g) provision for proposed dividends." [3] To this list of current liabilities we would add replacement provisions equivalent to oncoming and relatively current commitments for capital expenditure related to fixed asset replacements.

[1] Thus, part of the judgment in the case of Verner *v.* General and Commercial Investment Trust (1912), 106 L. T. 49, reads as follows : " Perhaps the shortest way of expressing the distinction which I am endeavouring to explain is to say that fixed capital may be sunk and lost, and yet that the excess of current receipts over current payments may be divided, but that floating or circulating capital must be kept up, as otherwise it will enter into and form part of such excess, in which case to divide such excess without deducting the capital which forms part of it will be contrary to law."

[2] Gee and Company (Publishers) Ltd., pp. 20 and 22.

[3] The Companies Act, 1947, has now modified the meaning of the word " provision." Thus Paragraph 1 (1) (a), First Schedule, Part IV (Paragraph 27, Eighth Schedule, Part IV, 1948 Act), defines " provision " in the following manner—

" (1) For the purposes of this schedule, unless the context otherwise requires—

We turn to the more particular notions which accountants have associated with the word "income", and we immediately think of the sense in which the term is used in the title "Income and Expenditure Account" as applied to certain non-trading concerns, and in theory, at least, to individuals. Thus Section 123 of the Companies Act of 1929 (Section 148 of 1948 Act), which deals with company accounts, specifically requires, in the case of a company not trading for profit, an income and expenditure account to be laid before the company in general meeting. In this view, income is largely synonymous with current incomings, and although in the case of non-trading concerns, and more specifically individuals,[1] it has a large measure of validity, it cannot be made applicable to trading enterprises without involving a highly artificial use of the term. Thus there is authority for suggesting that income as applied to trading enterprises is more commonly thought of in accounting usage as meaning operating profit, very largely in the sense of operating incomings minus associated operating outgoings.

(a) the expression 'provision' shall, subject to sub-paragraph (2) of this paragraph, mean any amount written off or retained by way of providing for depreciation, renewals or diminution in value of assets or retained by way of providing for any known liability of which the amount cannot be determined with substantial accuracy."

Sub-paragraph (2), referred to above, states that "where—

(a) any amount written off or retained by way of providing for depreciation, renewals or diminution in value of assets, not being an amount written off in relation to fixed assets before the coming into force of this schedule; or

(b) any amount retained by way of providing for any known liability;

is in excess of that which in the opinion of the directors is reasonably necessary for the purpose, the excess shall be treated for the purposes of this schedule as a reserve and not as a provision."

The Institute of Chartered Accountants has recently (May, 1948) pointed out that "The word 'provision' is commonly used in accounts in a much less restricted sense, as including, in addition to provisions as defined in paragraph 1 (1) (a), amounts provided for liabilities the amounts whereof can be closely estimated and for amounts not constituting 'known liabilities' (for example, deferred repairs). The definition in the schedule is more limited than that recommended by the Council in 1943 in paragraph 1 (b) of recommendation VI on reserves and provisions; under (i) of that paragraph 'provision' included amounts set aside to meet 'specific requirements the amounts whereof can be estimated closely.'"

According to the opinion of counsel obtained by the Institute it seems that "The expression 'provision' as used in the First Schedule is defined by paragraph 1 (1) (a), Part IV of that schedule and nothing that does not fall within that definition can in our opinion properly be described as a provision." Hence the Council of the Institute has now (May, 1948) recommended that "The word 'provision' should cease to be used to denote amounts set aside to meet specific requirements the amounts whereof can be estimated closely; such amounts should be grouped with creditors since they represent liabilities or accruals."

[1] The current incomings or income of an individual would be composed of all those ordinary sources which are noted on the common form of Income Tax return.

A leading American accountant has reminded us that income is a word of many meanings. He has said that

" in the terminology of manufacturing and trading it has displaced the older and more suggestive word, ' profit ' . . . the use of the terms ' profit ' and ' profit and loss account ' suggests the important truth that gain is usually a difference and must be measured by matching costs and expenses against revenue. This usage also provides a constant reminder of the fact that costs and expenses may exceed revenue and produce the loss that is the antithesis of profit. The sacrifice of significance resulting from the substitution of the word ' income ' is not justified by the slight gain in brevity. However, in the accounting field there seems to be a constant disposition to sacrifice accuracy to terseness, and in this case the tendency is so encouraged by the existence of income taxation that it is perhaps necessary to accept the newer terminology. The considerations recited, however, point to the desirability of adopting as the concept of income that which is suggested by the word ' profit '." [1]

In this quotation we discern something of the importance ascribed by accountants to the notion of income, in relation to business enterprise, as a process of matching operating outgoings against associated operating incomings. In accounting theory, this notion of business income is fundamental, but it is clear that difficulties are posed by the association of such outgoings with such incomings. Thus, Professors Paton and Littleton remind us that

" a cost is both an acquisition price and, perhaps after several intermediate conversions, a charge to revenue. In general, these phases appear in the order stated through a period of time. If the business enterprise itself were of short duration, or if business operations were of such a nature that all costs as incurred were immediately associated with realised revenue, the two aspects would be merged and would not require separate recognition. Under either of these conditions, in other words, a cost would represent simply an acquisition price to be compared with current revenue in the period in which the transaction occurred. Actually the typical business is a continuing process and income is a stream which must be broken up, for purposes of measurement and reporting, into convenient time-sections. Modern business operations, moreover, are so complex and require the use of such long-lived cost factors as to make the acceptance of this dual conception of cost essential to sound accounting. A cost is initially an acquisition price and only finally a deduction from revenue. The fundamental problem of accounting, therefore, is the division of the stream of costs incurred between the present and the future in the process of measuring periodic income." [2]

[1] *Financial Accounting*, by G. O. May (New York : The Macmillan Company, 1943, and used with their permission), pp. 25–26.

[2] *An Introduction to Corporate Accounting Standards*, by W. A. Paton and A. C. Littleton (American Accounting Association, 1940), pp. 66–67.

There is something in this which is not entirely dissimilar to the economic sense in which income has been conceived as a stream of useful goods and services, although that view of the matter by itself does not seem adequate. Perhaps economically it is better to look at income according to the concept of Mr. J. R. Hicks when he says that " the purpose of income calculations in practical affairs is to give people an indication of the amount which they can consume without impoverishing themselves. Following out this idea, it would seem that we ought to define a man's income as the maximum value which he can consume during a week, and still expect to be as well off at the end of the week as he was at the beginning. Thus, when a person saves, he plans to be better off in the future ; when he lives beyond his income, he plans to be worse off. Remembering that the practical purpose of income is to serve as a guide for prudent conduct, I think it is fairly clear that this is what the central meaning must be." [1]

This is an approach which largely commends itself to accounting minds, who all the way through have been trained to the view that income and savings impose the ultimate restraints on expenditure, and in our private capacities the hard school of experience has made us well aware of the troubles and difficulties we can lay up for ourselves if outgoings are allowed to exceed incomings, unless either we retard the one or push up the other and by so doing implicate ourselves in the conditions that those courses of action give rise to. In a rather more precise sense, most English accountants would not wish to regard income as necessarily co-terminous with operating profit. Businesses are so constituted as to have a main purpose and it is in relation to this main purpose that profit and loss accounts are first framed to measure " operating profit." Nevertheless, most businesses have subsidiary economic activities, together with a number of other activities which are purely financial in character, and which fall to be treated as non-operating incomings and outgoings. In general, therefore, it seems better to regard income in the sense of total profit, that is, the operating profit relevant to the main purpose for which the enterprise was constituted, the profits from the subsidiary economic activities, and the non-operating incomings less non-operating outgoings. It is this total profit [2] which for all practical purposes constitutes the income of an enterprise and which, after adjustment for extraneous and exceptional items, ordinarily requires to be judged in relation to capital employed in the course of determining whether or not that enterprise is earning a proper return from the resources which it has engaged in investment.

[1] *Value and Capital*, by J. R. Hicks, Second Edition (Oxford at the Clarendon Press, 1946), p. 172.

[2] It will be clear that this total profit is arrived at before providing for taxation.

We should also remark that there is a narrow sense in which accountants apply the word income to one particular classification of assets, even when they are considering business enterprises, as in the case of income from security investments, but usually it is clear from the context what is implied, and this incidental use of the term is not of sufficient importance to dwell on here. Problems sometimes arise on the dichotomy between operating and non-operating, a familiar example of which arises on the realisation of security investments. Whether or not a gain or loss on the realisation of security investments can be regarded as an operating one depends upon the intention evidenced by the particular constitution, and sometimes the practice, of the enterprise concerned ; an intention which on the one hand may involve dealing to earn or on the other hand holding to earn. Those enterprises which by intention professionally deal in security investments are normally regarded as operating a business through the purchase and sale of investments and such gains or losses as arise from this source are treated as operating. It is not without interest to notice that British taxation practice tends to impose a constraint on investment companies, that is, companies formed to hold investments for the purpose of earning income, by tacitly requiring that such gains as we have been considering be dealt with by appropriate transfer to capital reserve, on the authority of a constitutional direction which precludes their distribution as income.

III

THE NATURE OF PROFIT

IN a free enterprise economy the measurement of profit is a central feature of private accounting practice, and in the first chapter of this study we outlined some of the reasons why this was so. A primary necessity for short period reports of stewardship compelled a periodic measure, a view of the matter which was later reinforced by economic claims for periodic tests designed to reveal the effectiveness of the organisation of resources ; but a periodic measure requires certain conventions. In accounting usage business incomings and outgoings are not immediately related to the interests of proprietors. Instead they are thought of in terms of an institutional stream of continuing economic activities, as a result of which periodic statements of account are looked at from a standpoint which rests upon a fundamental assumption of continuity. Such an assumption is very largely a matter of convention for it is clear that nobody can quite foretell what is going to happen in the future with any strong degree of confidence. The concept of a normal stream of continuing activity is based upon the hope that an enterprise when once started is likely to be reasonably successful, for those persons who venture into a business do not usually begin by anticipating its liquidation. As a consequence accounts are not ordinarily prepared with this eventuality in mind, although an occasion may arise in which financial embarrassment is becoming so clearly apparent that the accountant must give due weight to the situation by anticipating its repercussions. But this aside, we have to face the fact that periodic reports of profits require that a continuous stream of activities be viewed, somewhat affectedly perhaps, as a series of time segments, a prospect which must involve systematic methods of accrual and expiry. Business men are inclined to think in terms of money and in the ordinary run of their conduct of an enterprise they are very largely concerned to maximise the money margin between their cost inputs and their revenue outputs. Thus, in the technique of profit measurement there is always a process which seeks to establish a correspondence between money costs and money revenues over relatively short periods of time.

The operating profit of an enterprise is thought of by accountants as the monetary gain arising to an enterprise as a result of its current working, and to safeguard its financial stability considerable care is taken not to anticipate this profit. So it comes about that a profit is not finally accounted until it has been realised either in terms of cash or what is regarded as equivalent—accruing money claims, except in certain peculiar circumstances in which a compromise has to be sought, as in the case of a firm which is engaged on a few large contracts of relatively long duration. In this view current money incomings constitute the pivot of the technique and a primary duty of the accountant is the ascertainment of those related money outgoings which promoted such incomings, that is, the cost of sales as these aggregated outgoings are called in the language of trading accounts. The margin between operating incomings and the associated operating outgoings as related to a given period of time is commonly the accounting measure of operating profit. The introduction of the element of periodicity into accounting statements involves conventional adjustments for it is quite plain that in most businesses there are likely to be current outgoings which are not immediately consummated by current incomings. Thus accountants carry over to the measure of profit of a succeeding period those operating outgoings which are not directly associated with the operating incomings of the current period. The ascertainment of the monetary value to be placed upon such outgoings can give rise to a number of practical problems for any sizable undertaking, but in the fundamental theory of accounting the elemental intention is to carry over all actual outgoings which cannot be conveniently associated with the operating incomings assignable to the time period for which a profit measure is sought.

Again, it is clear that in almost every business there are some outgoings which can only be assigned to the operating incomings of long periods which means that in assessing the profit of any one short period some way of expiring long dated outgoings against current operating incomings must be attempted. Familiar examples are found in those fixed assets, for example, plant and machinery, which come to be gradually used up during the course of manufacturing operations. The statement on Accounting Principles of the Institute of Chartered Accountants makes the point that " Fixed assets, whatever be their nature or the type of business in which they are employed, have the fundamental characteristic that they are held with the object of earning revenue and not for the purpose of sale in the ordinary course of business." [1] There is a clear distinction between a current operating outgoing which may be more or less immediately associated with a current operating incoming and an outgoing constituted by expenditure on a fixed asset which is likely to last for some time. The accounting association of a segment of that outgoing with current operating incomings is known as provision for depreciation, which for accountants " represents that part of the cost of a fixed asset to its owner

[1] *Recommendations on Accounting Principles*: IX.—Depreciation of Fixed Assets.

which is not recoverable when the asset is finally put out of use by him. Provision against this loss of capital is an integral cost of conducting the business during the effective commercial life of the asset and is not dependent upon the amount of profit earned." [1] Methods of accrual and expiry, in relation to both incomings and outgoings, have been adopted by accountants as reasonable means of setting operating accounts within a selected short time interval on a receivable expendable basis.

The notion of periodicity as related to the measurement of profit has not always been readily accepted, principally on the grounds that it is arbitrary, unnatural and artificial when judged against the background concept of continuity, but apart altogether from many other considerations [2] proprietors must have periodic reports of stewardship, particularly in these days of the divorce of ownership from management, and so too, managements must have some means of knowing the way they are going over comparatively short time intervals if they are to resist and correct those influences which are not making for a best distribution of resources. It has been well said in a rather different connection that

" Our bodily life is essentially periodic. It is dominated by the beatings of the heart, and the recurrence of breathing. The presupposition of periodicity is indeed fundamental to our very conception of life. We cannot imagine a course of nature in which, as events progressed, we should be unable to say : ' This has happened before.' The whole conception of experience as a guide to conduct would be absent. Men would always find themselves in new situations possessing no substratum of identity with anything in past history." [3]

---

[1] *Recommendations on Accounting Principles :* IX.—Depreciation of Fixed Assets.

[2] Mr. G. O. May gives ten major uses of accounting statements, of which he says the first five might be regarded as the older, and the second five as the more modern uses, and he regards the distinction between the two as significant. Those in the first group are :
    1. As a report of stewardship ;
    2. As a basis of fiscal policy ;
    3. To determine the legality of dividends ;
    4. As a guide to wise dividend action ;
    5. As a basis for the granting of credit.
Those in the second group are :
    6. As information for prospective investors in an enterprise ;
    7. As a guide to the value of investments already made ;
    8. As an aid to Government supervision ;
    9. As a basis for price or rate regulation ;
    10. As a basis for taxation.
Financial Accounting, pp. 19–21 (New York : The Macmillan Co., 1943, and used with their permission).

[3] *An Introduction to Mathematics*, by A. N. Whitehead, p. 165 (Oxford, 1945).

Nevertheless, there is a caution, as one accountant has been at some pains to remind us, and we must never forget that "Accounts are essentially historical records and, as is true of history in general, correct conclusions cannot be reached by a hurried survey of temporary conditions, but only by a longer retrospect and a careful distinction between permanent tendencies and transitory influences".[1] In other words the matters which tend to claim our attention in the preparation of periodical accounts by the nature of things are those which more often than not depend upon expedient short term considerations. The accounting bent towards conservatism was something of an attempt to correct this, though perhaps it was more governed by a sense of caution, and a perception gleaned from experience that nothing can be expected to go smoothly for long without some setbacks, than by a well formulated principle based on a conscious recognition of the effect of long term trends.

We may hope that by now we have said enough to show that the accounting measurement of the operating profit of a business enterprise is definable in terms of its current operating incomings derived from the monetary claims accruing in respect of the goods which it has delivered and the services which it has rendered over a given space of time, less its current operating outgoings conceived as the monetary claims which it has incurred in respect of goods received by delivery and services rendered in furtherance of its purposes during the same period of account, together with appropriate adjustments for proportionate allocations of long term outgoings, and inventories of current operating outgoings not immediately capable of association with the current operating incomings falling within the time period of profit ascertainment. But although accountants have built up their technique on the basis of a firm attachment to the business principle that input money costs are always incurred in the world of commerce with a recovery intention out of output money revenues, they have not entirely overlooked the deeper implications of the temporal relation between efforts and current achievements, of exertions and current realised benefits, though it cannot be denied that on balance they have allowed the former view to force its claim upon their attention, a situation which has provoked some odd problems in the attempt to associate past efforts with current benefits. Not unnaturally the accounting concepts of money cost recovery will always tend to bear upon the money end of things rather than upon the real goods and services, efforts and accomplishments, which pass against their monetary expressions, and for this reason we emphasise the point that when put to the assessment of an optimum utilisation of resources it may require to be treated warily.

[1] G. O. May, *Twenty-five Years of Accounting Responsibility*, p. 71 (American Institute Publishing Co., 1936).

40

Accountants distinguish positive and negative elements in the assessment of profit or loss. These appellations are, perhaps, a little unfortunate since the negatives are very largely the first causes of the positives, but they serve to emphasise the major accounting dichotomy to which we are directing our attention in this chapter. The negative elements, as we have partially noticed, are variously described as outgoings, costs, expendables or payables, debits or charges, and, in a rather more sophisticated connection, inputs ; while their positive counterparts are referred to as incomings, revenues, receivables, credits, and outputs. In the accounting technique of profit measurement these terms are used, consistently, in pairs ; thus costs are related to and associated with revenues, inputs with outputs, and, rather obviously, outgoings with incomings, payables with receivables, and debits with credits.

The accounting document which displays a period measure of profit is known in England as the profit and loss account, a title appropriate to the assessment of monetary residues resulting to proprietorship from economic activities. In America the similar document is more commonly described as the income statement, and having regard to later refinements in the analysis of the current account it is a title which cannot be lightly disregarded. In more recent years the structure of the accounting statement of classified entries on current account has undergone some modification. In England it is probable that some impetus was given to this development by the *Kylsant* case which did much to draw attention to the desirability of at least disclosing the *operating* earnings of public companies, besides throwing into prominence the unsatisfactory nature of undisclosed reserves. The Committee on Company Law Amendment which reported in June, 1945, specifically recommended that the profit and loss account should give a true and fair indication of the earnings or income of the period covered by the account and that it should disclose any material respects in which it included extraneous or non-recurrent transactions or transactions of an exceptional nature. This recommendation further provided that if in any such period a material change was made in the basis on which the account or any item therein was calculated, attention should be called to the change and to the effect thereof by way of note on the account.[1] Such a recommendation is significant of the trend in accounting thought on those questions which appertain to the income reports of business enterprises. The general tenor of this trend is marked by a design which virtually attempts a fundamental division of the current account into three parts. The first part is so framed as to lay the emphasis on the operating activities of the particular enterprise. It contains all those items to which we have already

[1] *Report of the Committee on Company Law Amendment*, p. 61.

drawn attention in the discussion on the accounting measurement of operating profit or loss, though at this stage it is perhaps well to make it clear that whereas the accountant, in the present stage of accounting technique, would very largely limit the items entering into this section in terms of a monetary dimension based on historical costs and historical revenues, the applied economist in his association with such a presentation would prefer a measure of operating profit or loss in which some attempt was made to counter the effect of changes in the value of money in so far as this can be specifically related to adjustments for depreciation and inventories.

It should be remarked that the operating section of the profit and loss account or income statement is related by intention to the main objects and purposes for which the enterprise was constituted. It will be apparent that many enterprises are engaged in subsidiary economic activities which yield profits or losses apart from the main activities. Such subsidiary profits or losses should be calculated and portrayed by means of separate and subsidiary operating accounts designed to support the residuary figures customarily set in the second part of the main statement. This second part will receive the main operating profit or loss of the enterprise and be followed by the subsidiary profits or losses arising from its lesser activities. Thereafter, it will take up the non-operating incomings and outgoings of the business on current account, entries which are very largely financial in character as in the very common example of income from security investments, to give the income of the enterprise. Within this part of the account we shall also find the extraneous, non-recurrent or exceptional items, relevant to the results of the period. Perhaps we might add that it is this distinction between operating profit and income which seems to give a preference to the title income statement.

The third section of the income statement should be designed in the form of an appropriation account to show how the income of the period derived from all the sources open to the particular enterprise is devoted to taxation, and dividends and withdrawals, to give the retained income or saving of the period. It may be strictly necessary to add a fourth section for the publication of abnormal credits or charges which turn out to be related to previous periods and to show any withdrawals from reserve in the form of past accumulated savings covering current withdrawals although in practice these items are conveniently dealt with by so arranging the appropriation account as to portray the totals of accumulated retained and unappropriated incomes at the beginning and end of the period of income measure.

In that part of the statement on accounting principles, issued by the Council of the Institute of Chartered Accountants, which dealt with the forms of balance sheet and profit and loss account it was said that " businesses are so varied in their nature that there must be flexibility in the manner of presenting accounts and a standard form to suit every commercial and industrial undertaking is neither practicable nor desirable." However much we may feel disposed to question this embargo on statistical uniformity, more particularly when it comes to the matter of national accounts, we must agree with the succeeding observations to the effect that " the financial position can, however, be more readily appreciated if the various items in the balance sheet are grouped under appropriate headings and a proper view of the trend of the results can be obtained only if certain principles are consistently applied and if profits or losses of an exceptional nature or relating to previous periods are stated separately in the profit and loss account." In relation to the discussion upon which we are embarked in this chapter it is the reference to the form of the profit and loss account which is significant, a reference which is more specifically enunciated in the following recommendation taken from the same source.

" The profit and loss account should be presented in such a form as to give a clear disclosure of the results of the period and the amount available for appropriation, for which purpose it may conveniently be divided into sections. Such a disclosure implies substantial uniformity in the accounting principles applied as between successive accounting periods ; any change of a material nature, such as a variation in the basis of stock valuation or in the method of providing for depreciation or taxation, should be disclosed if its effect distorts the results. The account should disclose any material respects in which it includes extraneous or non-recurrent items or those of an exceptional nature, and should also refer to the omission of any item relative to, or the inclusion of any item not relative to, the results of the period." [1]

Design of Accounts, a Research Committee publication of the Society of Incorporated Accountants which first appeared in 1944, also bore evidence to professional accounting developments in the statement of profit and loss accounts. It recommended that " published company revenue accounts should give a clear statement of operational profit, of non-operational items of income and expenditure, of provisions to meet liabilities defined as to time of accrual, of transfers to or from reserves clearly enunciated as such, and of the appropriation of residual balances. Every effort should be made to show the manner in which the true operational profit is built up." And again " accurately analysed revenue figures constitute a test of management, and in the case of published revenue accounts the share of each factor

---

[1] *Recommendations on Accounting Principles* by the Council of the Institute of Chartered Accountants : VIII—Form of Balance Sheet and Profit and Loss Account, particularly recommendations 16 and 17.

in production should be disclosed as well as the net amount available for the owners ".[1] Finally, we see these developments partially given the force of statutory provision in the Companies Act of 1947 with its requirements that

" every profit and loss account of a company shall give a true and fair view of the profit or loss of the company for the financial year ",[2] and that " there shall be shown : (a) the amount charged to revenue by way of provision for depreciation, renewals or diminution in value of fixed assets ; (b) the amount of the interest on the company's debentures and other fixed loans; (c) the amount of the charge for United Kingdom income tax and other United Kingdom taxation on profits, including, where practicable, as United Kingdom income tax any taxation imposed elsewhere to the extent of the relief, if any, from United Kingdom income tax and distinguishing where practicable between income tax and other taxation ; (d) the amounts respectively provided for redemption of share capital and for redemption of loans ; (e) the amount, if material, set aside or proposed to be set aside to, or withdrawn from, reserves ; (f) the amount, if material, set aside to provisions other than provisions for depreciation, renewals or diminution in value of assets or, as the case may be, the amount, if material, withdrawn from such provisions and not applied for the purposes thereof ; (g) the amount of income from investments, distinguishing between trade investments and other investments ; (h) the aggregate amount of the dividends paid and proposed."[3]

Moreover, the following matters are required to be stated by way of note to the profit and loss account, if not otherwise shown.

" (2) If depreciation or replacement of fixed assets is provided for by some method other than a depreciation charge or provision for renewals, or is not provided for, the method by which it is provided for or the fact that it is not provided for, as the case may be. (3) The basis on which the charge for United Kingdom income tax is computed. (4) Whether or not the amount stated for dividends paid and proposed is for dividends subject to deduction of income tax. (5) . . . the corresponding amounts for the immediately preceding financial year for all items shown in the profit and loss account. (6) Any material respects in which any items shown in the profit and loss account are affected—

    (a) by transactions of a sort not usually undertaken by the company or otherwise by circumstances of an exceptional or non-recurrent nature ; or

    (b) by any change in the basis of accounting ".[4]

[1] *Design of Accounts*, pp. 5–6 (Oxford University Press, 1944).

[2] Section 13 (1) (Section 149.—(1), 1948 Act).

[3] First Schedule B 8 (1) (Eighth Schedule 12.—(1), 1948 Act).

[4] First Schedule B—Profit and Loss Account, 9 (1)–(6) (Eighth Schedule, 14—(1)–(6), 1948 Act).

We may notice by way of comment on these provisions which we have cited from the Companies Act of 1947, that much emphasis is placed, and in our view rightly placed, on exposing to view a class of transaction which might be described as relevant to the non-operating part, either positive or negative, of a company's income, including " transactions of a sort not usually undertaken by the company or otherwise by circumstances of an exceptional or non-recurrent nature." That there should be a growing social consciousness of the necessity for reasonable disclosure in the publication of company accounts is all to the good, but with such a marked stress on the one part of a company's current account in the interests of shareholding proprietors, it cannot but strike the impartial observer as a little odd that no such requirements have been thought essential to cover the highly significant make-up of a company's operating account, more particularly when we come to regard the evident importance attached to the separate statement (aside from what should be its logical context) of " amounts charged to revenue by way of provision for depreciation, renewals or diminution in value of fixed assets." This wears an air of but half a story, and whatever the expedient arguments adduced to convince the legislature, presumably on the over-pressed score of protecting competing interests, we are sometimes tempted into feeling that at least one great opportune step to further the cause of such economic inquiries as are directed to the service of over-all financial stability has been lost by this failure to provide for a reasonable portrayal of the working account. Yet again, we may ask, what is the real objective significance attaching to the disclosure of an item of so called profit which is before charging or crediting a number of other operating and non-operating items specifically required to be separately stated under the Act ? By itself, whatever the purpose sought, such a figure is plainly ambiguous when judged from the standpoint of any acceptable accounting definition of operating surplus.

But there is another side to all this which the members of the Committee on Company Law Amendment were at some pains to point out, and maybe it is the better way, if only it could be treated with the urgency which it deserves. Perhaps the exigencies of our latter day plight may impel us to pursue it. Thus, at paragraph 97, page 54, of the Report presented by the President of the Board of Trade to Parliament in June, 1945, it was made clear that the Committee had considered suggestions, directed to the assistance of those responsible for framing general economic policy, and which required that companies should

" disclose in their accounts details of sales, expenses of production, selling and distribution, administration and management, and other like details. In our view," so ran the Committee's Report, " such information could not be given in sufficient detail to achieve the object in view without loading the published accounts, of which the primary purpose is to convey financial information in a form that can be assimilated by shareholders and creditors, with so much detail as to fail in that purpose. We consider that information required for general economic purposes would be more appropriately and conveniently obtained through some such machinery as the Census of Production Act, under which information could be required in greater detail than would be practicable in published accounts."

In the circumstances of the times it may well be that the machinery of the Census of Production Act is the better instrument to the fulfilment of national economic inquiries, but even such an instrument is not free from the immediate requirement of adaptation to the growing technique of Social Accounting.

As we look at all these various professional accounting developments relevant to the statement of the profit and loss account we cannot fail to be impressed by the merit ascribed to vertical or periodical uniformity, and which reaches its quintessence in the recommendation that company profit and loss accounts should disclose any material respects in which they include extraneous or non-recurrent transactions or those of an exceptional nature, and that due indication should be made of any material change made in the basis on which the accounts have been prepared or any item therein has been calculated, with appropriate reference to the effect on the period measure of profit. By such means comparisons between the periodical income statements of the same unit are made secure. Apart, however, from statements of an order which require that a profit and loss account shall show the true profit for a period of account, or that it shall be presented in such a form as to give a clear disclosure of the results of the period, or again, in the words of the statute,[1] that it shall give a true and fair view of the profit or loss of the financial year, there seems to have been a somewhat tacit sidestepping of the merits of horizontal uniformity as might be thought of by a conforming shape for *all* enterprise accounts. No doubt the reasons are not far to seek, for one thing it involves the thorny problem of standardisation, and for another it implies some degree of uniformity in the bases of measurement of contentious items, let alone some troublesome considerations of publicity. Standardisation has long been looked upon askance by some members of the accounting profession, for perhaps it may have seemed to carry a totalitarian tinge of disconcerting hue, and refuge has been sought in assertions which assign impracticability to a course which must face the intricacies inherent in the diversity which is of the very nature of business enterprise, with the afterthought that standardised forms might restrict further progress in the development of accounting technique. But we shall never set our course

---

[1] The Companies Act, 1947 (and 1948).

aright in this era of malaise without some attention to its merits, for national accounts based on the aggregation of relatively standardised private accounts, with undue publicity safeguarded by a careful attention to the principles of confidentiality, are essential if the effects of the economic conduct of the nation both now and in the future are to be looked upon in much the same way as those which influence the well-being of a private firm. Clearly this is a matter of some consequence to all of us for properly interpreted national accounts must ultimately redound to the benefit of each individual firm operating within the economy.

This seems a convenient point at which to permit ourselves a second notice of the common accountancy practice which earmarks retained profits to general reserve accounts, a practice presumably entered into with the window dressing object of limiting dividend distributions to company shareholders and the withdrawals of proprietors. We have discerned from the quotations indicative of recent professional accounting developments that importance is assigned to the disclosure of transfers to and from reserves, whether general or specific, in relation to their effect on the statement of income available for distribution, the implications of which may have led us to reflect on whether or not this game of labelling business savings as a means to their constitutional retention is really worth the candle. Two prominent requirements of any balance sheet are the amounts of the contributed money capital, and the income accumulations strictly interpreted as savings. In the form of some past balance sheets we had frequently to resort to an addition sum in order to determine the latter figure. If for some purposes we should wish to measure real savings then the application of money savings to asset formation becomes important, for in so far as savings have financed increases in money claims their figure statement will not be affected by changes in the value of money. In so far as savings have financed increases in real assets, they should present problems of revaluation in money terms, though this is far from being an acceptable accounting tenet.

As we noticed in the previous chapter, the accounting and constitutional variants imposed on the statement of accumulated income have not gone unquestioned. Thus Professors Paton and Littleton assert quite plainly that

" The process of subdividing surplus and of returning true surplus reserves to general surplus account should not be considered a part of the accounting for income and hence should not be permitted to affect the income statement. It should hardly be necessary to add that surplus reserves should be clearly distinguished from liability ' reserves ' and accounts showing accrued depreciation and other offsets to the asset costs." [1]

[1] Op. cit., p. 109.

47

It remains for us to add that for our part we are concerned to impose qualities of strength and clarity upon the concepts of accumulated savings, and the retained income or saving of a given period of account, regarding the former as the sum of the retained income of the past up to the beginning of the accounting period at the close of which a balance sheet is drawn.

If, as some economists have implied, we are to regard enterprise income in terms of the outputs of useful goods and services which flow from an efficient organisation of real assets appropriately supported by a counterpoised labour force, then it cannot be doubted that precise attempts at quantitative profit measurements are dependent upon quantitative measurements of maintainable real capital. Another view expresses the matter somewhat differently by defining income as that amount available for consumption expenditure which leaves an enterprise, or person for that matter, as well off at the end as at the beginning of a period of account. There are even some English legal decisions which appear to support this approach. For example, in the case of *In re The Spanish Prospecting Co. Ltd.* decided in the Court of Appeal in November, 1910,[1] Lord Justice Fletcher Moulton said in the course of his judgment that

" the word ' profits ' has, in my opinion, a well-defined meaning, and this meaning coincides with the fundamental conception of ' profits ' in general parlance, although in mercantile phraseology the word may at times bear meanings indicated by the special context, which deviate in some respects from the fundamental signification. ' Profits ' implies comparison between the state of a business at two specific dates, usually separated by an interval of a year. The fundamental meaning is the amount of gain made by the business during the year. This can only be ascertained by a comparison of the assets of the business at the two dates."

A little later on in the same judgment it is stated quite firmly that

" we start, therefore, with this fundamental definition of ' profits,' viz. if the total assets of the business at the two dates be compared with the increase which they show at the later date as compared with the earlier date (due allowance, of course, being made for any capital introduced into or taken out of the business in the meanwhile) represents in strictness the profits of the business during the period in question."

Nevertheless, we must be on our guard against reading into this judgment any necessarily coincident economic view of profit, for we may have noticed the introduction of a reference to capital which by implication suggests money capital, and in point of fact the general run of English case law which skirts this subject is much concerned with another principle, fundamental to the specifically legal approach, which looks to the protection of contributed money capital rather

[1] Acct. L.R., 17th December, 1910.

48

than to the safeguarding of the underlying real asset formation.[1] It is this other legal view which has tended to weigh heavily upon the development of accounting conventions, for quite naturally accounting documents are taken to evidence business conduct in the use of proprietorship money, and it is taken for granted by the business community that they will conform to a legal expectation which, at bottom, has informed the greater part of English company legislation. It is therefore not surprising that accountants have primarily felt themselves called upon to measure the income of a corporate enterprise, or for that matter any other form of enterprise, in terms of a strict revelation of the manner in which *money* capital has been maintained, while at the same time communicating to the proprietors the amount of additional money gained, which, having regard to the law, they may safely look upon as available for distribution to the satisfaction of their personal and several necessities. Thus it comes about that only in comparatively recent times, co-existent with a rise in national economic consciousness, have economic concepts of income presented themselves to accountants as in any way claiming their attention.

At this point in our discussion we may begin to detect something of the nature of those expedients of convenience which pass under the general designation of accounting convention, as well as some of the reasons why they have grown up in the form in which we now know them. For example it is not difficult to see a superior cause of the orientation of accounting convention to the preservation of the contributed money capital of proprietors, and the money claims of creditors, as having deeply laid roots in those speculative disturbances which reach at least as far back as the early eighteenth century. In fact, as we have hinted elsewhere,[2] professional accounting technique as we know it to-day, owes a great deal to its upbringing in intimate association with the administration of the bankruptcy and company laws.

The principle of adequate disclosure in the interests of shareholders and creditors is still the dominant motive in the accounting provisions of company law, a principle which, by limitation to the one section of the social conscience which it seeks to serve, has, in the Companies Act of 1947 (and the Act of 1948), as it seems to some of us, unwittingly gone to the length of distorting the presentation and logical ordering of published company accounts. In this connection it is instructive to turn to the opening paragraphs of that part of the *Report of the Com-*

---

[1] For an inquiry into the English legal decisions which concern the Measurement of Profit the reader is referred to the writer's *Precision and Design in Accountancy*, p. 60 (Gee and Company (Publishers) Ltd., 1947).

[2] *Precision and Design in Accountancy*, p. 43, Chapter on the Development in the Functions of Accountants (Gee and Company (Publishers) Ltd., 1947).

mittee on Company Law Amendment [1] which deals with accounts. At the risk of some repetition, we take the liberty of quoting them here in full.

" 96. General.—The history of company legislation shows *the increasing importance attached to publicity in connection with accounts.* The Act of 1862 contained no compulsory provisions with regard to audit or accounts, though Table A to that Act did include certain clauses dealing with both matters. In 1879 provision was made for the audit of the accounts of banking companies but it was not until 1900 that any such provision was made generally applicable. It was only on 1st July, 1908, when the Companies Act, 1907, came into force, that provision was made for including a statement in the form of a balance sheet in the annual return to the Registrar of Companies, and that provision exempted private companies from this requirement. The Act now in force requires directors to produce a balance sheet and a profit and loss account in every calendar year and to *lay them before the company in general meeting.* The Act lays down some requirements as to the contents of the balance sheet ; we refer to them in greater detail in paragraph 99. But there are no requirements as to the form of the profit and loss, or income and expenditure, account, nor does the Act in terms make the auditor's report cover the profit and loss account, though, since the balance on that account is necessarily carried into the balance sheet, an auditor cannot discharge his duties without examining it. We consider that the profit and loss account is as important as, if not more important than, the balance sheet, since the trend of profits is the best indication of the prosperity of the company and the value of the assets depends largely on the maintenance of the business as a going concern."

" 97. Present practice.—The amount of *information disclosed* in the accounts of companies varies widely. The recent tendency has been to give more information and this tendency has been fortified by the valuable recommendations published from time to time by the responsible accountancy bodies as to the form in which accounts should be drawn up and the information which they should contain. The directors of many, but by no means all, companies now give *shareholders* as much information as they consider practicable and the accounts which they present contain much more detail than is required by law. Auditors use their influence to persuade directors to present their accounts in accordance with the principles laid down by the professional bodies to which they belong, but in the absence of statutory requirements they cannot override the directors and in some cases may be deterred from pressing their views by fear of losing their position as auditors. The professional bodies representing the accountants who gave evidence before us all agreed that the position of auditors would be strengthened if the law were to prescribe *a minimum amount of information to be disclosed* in all balance sheets and profit and loss accounts. We accept this view and have considered whether,

[1] H.M. Stationery Office—June, 1945.

as in the case of societies operating under the Friendly Societies Acts, Industrial Assurance Acts, Building Societies Acts and Industrial and Provident Societies Acts, there should not be prescribed forms of accounts with which all companies registered under the Companies Acts would be required to comply. In our view the diversity of companies is such that it is doubtful whether standard forms of accounts would be practicable and in any event we fear that standard forms might restrict further progress in the technique of *conveying information* through the published accounts. We have also considered suggestions that, to assist those responsible for framing general economic policy, companies should be required to disclose in their accounts details of sales, expenses of production, selling and distribution, administration and management, and other like details. In our view, however, such information could not be given in sufficient detail to achieve the object in view without loading the published accounts, *of which the primary purpose is to convey financial information in a form that can be assimilated by shareholders and creditors*, with so much detail as to fail in that purpose. We consider that *information required for general economic purposes* would be more appropriately and conveniently obtained through some such machinery as the Census of Production Act, under which information could be required in greater detail than would be practicable in published accounts." (Italics ours.)

This survey of company accounting practice is one of the best statements on the existing situation, and it will be noted that even with legislation as it now stands [1] there is still some measure of freedom left to directors so far as concerns the presentation of company accounts, provided that they do disclose such matters as the legislature regards as fulfilling the primary purpose of conveying *financial* information to *shareholders* and *creditors* in a form in which they can readily assimilate it. Nevertheless we cannot fail to notice that the Cohen Committee was still very largely preoccupied with such a presentation of published company accounts as would reveal how far those responsible for the conduct of a company's affairs had safeguarded the contributed money capital of proprietors and the monetary claims of creditors. The whole affair was looked upon as primarily a financial matter, and no doubt this is a very proper view so long as we chose to limit our perspective to the purely financial ends of individual enterprise. Once we accept this limitation we can see a very good show of reason to validate those conventions of account so well set forth in the Recommendations on Accounting Principles of the Institute of Chartered Accountants in England and Wales. [2]

But there is a hint of change. We can see it in the very fact that the Committee on Company Law Amendment did at least consider suggestions designed to relate accounts to the general economic policy

[1] Cf. The Companies Acts, 1947 and 1948.

[2] London : Gee and Company (Publishers) Ltd.

of the nation. It is true that this Committee did consider that information required for general economic purposes would be more appropriately and conveniently obtained through some such machinery as the Census of Production, and with this view we can have no quarrel. The important point to notice, however, is the maturing regard for the *economic* significance of accounting statements, a quantitative development which has very largely followed on Lord Keynes' deep interest in practical problems as related to the propositions of pure economics.

In an article on Lord Keynes contributed to *Nature* Mr. J. R. N. Stone wrote—

"Keynes' most sustained contribution to economics lay in the field of what used to be called the theory of money but which has been transformed into a wider and more connected subject through his labours. He directed attention away from the purely monetary aspect of this subject towards an analysis of all the factors determining the level of aggregate demand for goods and services. In analysing effective demand he laid stress on the distinction between consumption expenditure and expenditure on additions to wealth or capital formation, or, in his terminology, investment. The concept of expenditure has to do with spending on goods and services ; in addition, there is needed a concept of outlay which has to do with the disposal of income and may be divided into consumption outlay and saving. Now while the outlay and expenditure on consumption goods and services go hand-in-hand, a decision to save on the part of one individual does not automatically carry with it a desire to use that saving for investment purposes, since investment expenditure is in general undertaken by a set of individuals and businesses different from those undertaking the saving. From the definitions employed it follows that total saving is identically equal to total investment ; but Keynes showed that under conditions where there is a tendency to excess saving, that is, where the amount which the community wishes to save at the full employment level of income exceeds the amount which is wanted for investment purposes in the same circumstances, an equilibrium level of saving and investment might be brought about by a reduction in income and therefore in saving, rather than by any factor in the situation tending automatically to raise investment demands to the level of full employment saving. He further argued that the former mode of adjustment would be the normal one in modern economic societies, and that an equilibrium situation could exist and might be expected at a level of income well below that which would accompany the full employment of resources."

To make the matter clear to accountants we claim leave to add to our quotation from Mr. Stone's article.

"What, it may be asked, was new in all this ? How did Keynes' theories differ from the many theories of the trade cycle that had already made their appearance ? The gist of the answer to this question may perhaps be seen from the following considerations. First, he

52

aimed at what, mathematically speaking, was a complete explanation of the phenomena studied and did not concentrate, as many previous writers had done, on one particular phase of the trade cycle. Secondly, he *linked together the real and the monetary* aspects of the problem and found a place in his theories for confidence, expectations and similar psychological reactions, thus avoiding an explanation restricted to any one of these categories. Thirdly, he linked together the factors responsible for short-period changes with those operating to determine the average levels of the variables over longer periods, and showed that these average levels are also *dependent on the quantitative responses of the system*. The importance of this finding is that there is nothing in the mechanism of change in economic systems as we know them to make the equilibrium level an optimum level; in other words, the norm of a system in terms of employment may be any fraction of capacity, and there is nothing tending to bring the system automatically to a full use of capacity ".[1] (Italics ours.)

Thus the maintenance of aggregate demand to implicate a full use of productive resources is shown to be an essential objective of national economic and financial policy. National or social accounting is the attempt to present an overall picture of the transactions of a particular economy, relevant to a given period of account, which link together their real and monetary aspects, and thereby sets out to resolve those essential identities which may be utilised to reveal the means to the achievement of such an equilibrium situation as will promote a level of income consistent with a full employment of resources. As we have urged elsewhere [2] national or social accounting does very largely resolve itself into a matter of the aggregation of private accounting statements, particularly when it comes to the business enterprise sector of the national economy, and if forms of private accounting statements are to be devised which serve this purpose, it is clear that they must be prepared with a due regard for economic concepts.

The relevance of this over-all financial accounting approach is made abundantly plain by Professor Lionel Robbins in the last of his Marshall Lectures delivered at Cambridge in 1947 under the title of " The Economic Problem in Peace and War." Professor Robbins argues that

" for the avoidance of both inflation and deflation, I favour something which, if you like, you can call over-all financial planning. At the beginning of each appropriate period the government should make estimates both of the amount of expenditure (consumption plus investment) which is needed to maintain aggregate demand on a more

[1] *Lord Keynes: The New Theory of Money*, by J. R. N. Stone, *Nature*, Vol. 158, p. 652, 9th November, 1946.

[2] *Social Accounts and the Business Enterprise Sector of the National Economy* (shortly to be published by the Cambridge University Press).

or less even keel and of the amount of expenditure which is likely to be forthcoming. Then if there is a discrepancy between the two, either by way of a tendency to a rise or a fall in aggregate expenditure, it should seek, by what measures seem appropriate in that particular situation, to cause it to disappear. In the sector of public investment (which is likely henceforward to be large) it will have to plan in the current sense of the term, *as must any entrepreneur charged with the outlay of money.* The sector of public consumption (roughly the expenditure side of the budget) is likewise susceptible to direct control. At the same time in the private sectors, both of investment and consumption, there are available a considerable number of indirect controls, chiefly of a fiscal nature, which can be used, at discretion, to supplement these more direct measures. I am not quite sure whether a policy of this sort, which is designed to maintain over-all stability of aggregate demand, while leaving the maximum flexibility between the various constituent items, is correctly to be described by the term planning ; for, in current usage, that term has become more and more associated with other meanings. But on the assumption that the real meaning of the word to plan is to attempt to act with foresight and intelligence, I see no reason to refrain from staking a claim to its use. Why on earth should we refrain from designating as planning policies which are likely to be effective and coherent while retaining it for policies which are not likely to have these qualities ? At all events, I am convinced that, whatever else is done, a policy of this sort is incumbent on government." [1]   (Italics ours.)

Whatever views we may countenance for the term planning we cannot get away from the fact that this way of doing things is not so very unlike the technique of standard costing and flexible budgeting which has become so familiar a feature in modern accounting, and which has assigned to itself the role of a guide to those executives who are intimately concerned with the problems inevitably associated with the management of productive enterprise. It is doing for the nation what every intelligent entrepreneur does for his own enterprise, and as Professor Robbins goes on to say—

" The important thing is not that at every moment we should be in an exact state of ideal distribution of resources, but that in a broad way there should be no obstacles causing gross divergencies and that our organisation should be such as to afford the maximum scope for continual progress by way of cost reduction and innovation." [2]

We have designedly left it to the economists to speak for themselves, but accountants will not pass unnoticed the important implications of national accounting to which such approaches to economic problems point. Thus no accountant should wish to stand outside this field

[1] *The Economic Problem in Peace and War*, by Lionel Robbins, pp. 68–69 (London: Macmillan, 1947).

[2] Op. cit., p. 79.

of inquiry, and complacently assert—" With this I have no concern."
If he does so, then he refuses to recognise that the accounting profession
has any sense of mission, and, as a mere technical expert, he must
remain content with the conservative and narrow confines of the
mechanism of his craft. Just so soon as accountants do conceive the
uses of accounting forms for national economic purposes, even though
they be prepared quite independent of those which serve traditional
purposes, then they are bound to re-examine and call into question
the adequacy of such conventions as were subconsciously set to the
service of those traditional ends. Moreover, this over-all approach
is not necessarily so inconsistent with that of the individual enterprise,
as we shall see when we come to deal with such questions as provision
for depreciation and inventory valuation, and whichever way we look
at the matter we cannot get away from the fact that a proper and
reasonable measure of profit which takes into account underlying
productive realities is an income factor of the highest importance
both for the welfare of the individual firm and the national economy
as a whole. Surely there can be no doubt that the concept of the
maintenance of real capital as worked out by the pure economist is
one of the greatest importance for business well-being, more particularly
in a world marked by such economic uncertainty as to cast around
it the forbidding shadow of inflation. In such a situation it is only
to be expected that existing accounting conventions conceived in an
era of relative monetary stability should be strained and that their
validity should lose some force when brought to the test in a world
of change.

Accountants have been much exercised on questions which concern
the source of profit and the time of profit, and they frequently resort
to conventional compromises to resolve them. The device of separating
the operating account into two sections, the one to show the manufacturing results and the other the merchanting results, was an early
attempt to come to grips with this problem. Thus in a text-book
familiar to successive decades of accountancy students we read—

" When the commodities sold are actually manufactured by the business
instead of being purchased for the purpose of sale, the Trading Account
is better shown in two portions, called the Manufacturing Account and
Trading Account, respectively. The Manufacturing Account deals
with the cost of manufacturing the goods, the Trading Account
with the Sales and Gross Profit. The credit to the Manufacturing
Account in respect of finished goods can be treated in two ways :
(1) the manufactured goods are transferred to the Trading Account
at cost, i.e. cost of raw materials used plus manufacturing expenses ;
(2) the manufactured goods are transferred to the Trading Account
at market price and *a profit or loss on manufacturing* is shown. (Where
this method is used, a reserve will have to be made to eliminate the
unrealised profit from the closing stock, by debiting Profit and Loss

Account and crediting a Stock Reserve, otherwise the profits and stock will both appear at inflated figures in the Balance Sheet.) " [1] (Italics ours.)

The same points are taken in Cropper's *Higher Book-keeping and Accounts*:

" . . . a Manufacturing Account is prepared which is strictly confined to ascertaining the actual cost of the goods made, without reference to the current market price of similar goods. Then the account shows neither profit nor loss, and the balance, representing cost, is transferred to a Trading Account which includes sales and the relative distribution costs. . . . In yet other cases, the Manufacturing Account is charged with all costs of production on the usual lines, and is credited, at current market values, with the goods produced. The resulting balance shows the manufacturer's factory profit or loss on the basis of current market prices." [2]

Both quotations reveal alternative treatments. In the first proposal common to both, profits are quite clearly related to the conversion of input expenditure into *realised output* in terms of cash or debts due by customers. Thus profits are only recognised when they give rise to financial claims in respect of actual sales. This at once brings us to the fundamental accounting concept of " cost of sales." This concept quite plainly seeks to isolate expenditure on goods delivered and services rendered *to* an enterprise with a view to matching it with revenue from goods delivered and sold, and the services rendered *by* an enterprise, over a given period of time. But so far as current accounting practice goes, it is seldom that the cost of goods sold is extended to cover the charges which normally find their way into a business profit and loss account, and more often than not it does include a number of factory standing charges by reason of the accident of their debit in the so called manufacturing account. The concept of " cost of sales " is still very closely bound up with the merchanting notion of gross profit, about which we shall have more to say presently. We may add, however, that in at least one quarter considerable doubt has been thrown on the use of such a central concept of modern accounting procedure. Thus an American writer draws attention to the figure which the cost accountant in his country labels " cost of goods manufactured." He remarks that

" when this figure turns out to be higher than it was in a former period, management leaps to action (probably weeks or months after the damage has been started) ; armed with this figure, the determination of selling price becomes incredibly easy—just add 40 per cent. ; this

[1] *Book-keeping and Accounts*, by E. E. Spicer and E. C. Pegler, Tenth Edition edited by W. W. Bigg and H. A. R. J. Wilson, p. 18 (London : Pitman, 1938).

[2] *Higher Book-keeping and Accounts*, by L. Cuthbert Cropper, Fifth Edition pp. 14–15 (London : Macdonald and Evans, 1941).

figure, when found to be higher than the price at which the same product could be purchased on the outside, gives what is presumed to be clear indication of the proper course of action ; too large a portion of the wartime government contract decisions centered around this figure in their making." [1]

The fact that a cost of sales figure is not properly related to the measurement of operating profit in terms of realisation by reference to actual sales, but to a very early and out of date merchanting concept of gross profit, and to the fact that it is frequently used in much too rough and ready a way to set selling prices, leads us to regard it as a relatively unsatisfactory concept.

" Many times it has been stated that one of the fundamental purposes of cost accounting is to assist in the setting of sales prices. So strongly has this point been emphasised that it has, in the minds of many, come to be viewed as one of the routine continuing purposes of cost accounting—a purpose which is so continuously important that the design of the accounting system should reflect this as a major aim. The Committee,[2] on the other hand, believes that product pricing actually should be placed in a relatively subordinate position ; that it should be considered as one of the special services requiring special cost compilations. It is felt that the all too common belief that selling prices should be determined by adding a ' gross-profit ' margin to factory cost represents a reversal of the proper usage of the factory cost figure. Thus, while it may be reasonable, with proper reservations, to subtract a unit-cost figure from the actual sales price to arrive at net income, it is not reasonable to do the reverse—that is, to start with the unit cost and add a profit margin to arrive at a proposed selling price." [3]

It will be seen that we have identified the expression " cost of sales " with the factory cost of completed goods adjusted by the change in the opening and closing inventories of completed goods, but that by so doing within the structure of current accounting practice we emphasise the close allegiance of the concept with that relatively primitive conception—gross profit on sales.

To resume our discussion on the source and time of profit we see that the second account-keeping proposal, in the quotations from the text-books we cited, traces back to a manufacturing source so as to distinguish manufacturing profit from selling profit, although it still holds that the total realised profit of the enterprise is only consummated at the point of actual sale. Hence the need for the stock adjustment which we observe in the quotation from Spicer and Pegler's

---

[1] *Cost Concepts : Special Problems and Definitions*, by Robert L. Dixon (*The Accounting Review*, January, 1948, pp. 40–41).

[2] The Committee on Cost Concepts of the American Accounting Association.

[3] *Ibid.*, p. 41.

Book-keeping and Accounts. We may notice too the necessity to introduce the convention of a current external worth for goods manufactured in order to arrive at a manufacturing profit.

But peculiar problems can present themselves as soon as we try to measure profits at their productive sources. The productive process is continuous and any accounting statement about it only covers an arbitrary time period during which the whole of a cycle of operations will not have been completed. The necessity for a time allocation of costs is clearly recognised, but so too there is a necessity for a time allocation of benefits although it is not so easy in the case of a major work contract to put a current external worth measure on its uncompleted state, in order to identify the profit generation with the continuing productive process. The certainty of money profit measure only resolves itself when the work is completed, the time when total expenditure can be compared with total revenue to throw up the realised profit as a differential. Nevertheless if the principles of standard costing and flexible budgeting are followed in this particular context it should be possible to detect the probable and anticipated measure of the final review of expenditure and revenue, and by so doing to attach a current worth figure to uncompleted work in proportion to the amount of the effective costs incurred at the accounting date, leaving the ineffective costs (i.e. avoidable losses) to be set off against the provisional time period measure, to give the nearest possible estimate of operating profit based on source rather than on time of realisation. This can be a question of some moment for economists when they seek to prepare profit statements on an " industry " basis. Thus where there are several companies in a group, each of which is concerned with a different productive process, it could so happen, as a matter of group policy, that materials and goods in process were made to pass from one concern to another within the same group at cost rather than market value with the consequence that the profit on ultimate sale would accrue to the final concern in the chain, and would not necessarily be apportioned between concerns at different stages of the productive process. From the standpoint of the proprietorship interests of the group, this procedure is not objectionable if the ownership of each concern is identical, but it does set the economist, who would like to prepare his profit statements on an " industry " basis, an awkward problem. Thus, in this context, he would like to see operating profits brought into alignment with the productive processes, and for this purpose he would wish to see the transfers of products between fundamentally different processes carried through at market prices. It is not difficult to see that this is but another side to those problems which concern the source and time of profit. Mr. G. O. May has summed up the matter thus :

" The completion of the sale of a product may determine the time

58

of the making of a profit, but *not* its source. The real source of profit in a manufacturing business is the organisation and employment of capital and labour in the conversion of goods, selling is the realisation of the profit rather than the source. The amount of profit is affected by the degree of efficiency of the methods of realisation, just as it is affected by the degree of efficiency of the capital assets and the labour employed in production, and it is entirely equitable that there should be attributable to sale some part (but certainly not the whole) of the profit. . . . There is no profit until the goods have been both manufactured and sold." [1]

We have now to face a set of problems which depends upon the behaviour of cost inputs in relation to changes in revenue outputs. One of the most vital accounting distinctions is between those costs which may be classified as fixed or standing and those which may be regarded as moving or variable. This is a matter of particular importance when it comes to questions which concern the allocation of costs to production centres and ultimately to units of output, undertaken with the objects of controlling expenditure and eliminating such internal inefficiencies as are within the competence of those responsible for the management of an enterprise, and of guiding operating policy. The point must be made, however, that notwithstanding the existence of a highly developed costing accounting system designed to serve the objects we have mentioned, the system, by itself, cannot do more than set a course which indicates the best possible use of such resources as a firm happens to have available. This is clearly an internal affair, but whether or not a firm is employing the best possible resources it could to minimise its costs is still a matter which can only be resolved by reference to some external standards of performance, presumably those of the most efficient firm in the industry. Seemingly no one would yet deny that given freely competitive conditions this firm might be detected by the use of such an accounting ratio as that of operating profit to capital employed, calculating operating profit in the sense in which we are putting it forward in this book, and treating capital employed on the basis of the current value of the net assets at the beginning of the relevant accounting period.

It is difficult for industrial accountants, and for that matter professional accountants too, not to be carried away by the marked development in the technique of cost accounting which our generation has witnessed, but this enthusiasm must not be taken to the lengths of discrediting the financial accounts. Financial accounting forms are still of the most fundamental importance and this is particularly noticeable when they come to be related to the requirements of social or national accounting, for there, money flows in terms of the factors

---

[1] *Twenty-five Years of Accounting Responsibility*, by G. O. May, pp. 265–266 (The American Institute Publishing Co., 1936).

of production are the vital issues. The normal financial accounts of an enterprise are designed to give a *natural* over-all view of its economic transactions ; the cost accounts are designed to give sectional perspectives for the purpose of showing those who are concerned with management, the effectiveness or ineffectiveness of specific departments, or processes of production and to help them watch over controllable deviations from empirical standards of probable performance. But even " the technique of standard costing, coupled with budgetary control, requires complete integration of cost and financial records . . . the integration of cost and financial records is not merely advisable but is essential if the future development of cost accounting is to satisfy the needs of management ".[1] The cost accounts should arrive at the same total measure of operating profit as the financial accounts, and clearly for this purpose they should normally follow the same bases of measurement, although there may be an exceptional case in which the over-all and particular views are not necessarily coincident in the aggregate. We shall look at a possible example of this exception when we come to consider the influence of fixed expenses on inventory valuation.

From what has been said it will be seen that because cost accounting has been brought to maturity as a particular instrument of management it can never achieve quite the same general significance as financial accounting, and even when it does keep to its proper function it has still limitations which necessarily arise out of its dependence upon arbitrary conventions, some of which are overdue for a tidy up. Nevertheless reliable cost accounting has a very definite place in the scheme of an economy particularly if we assume ideals of uniformity of method, and the free exchange of information, within an industry. Once we have discovered the minimum cost producer, by the use of some such indicator as we have mentioned, then his cost accounting standards of performance can be applied by the other and more marginal producers in their own organisations. In such a way it might well be possible to achieve a best use of the resources which an industry should be able to command.

In accounting terminology connected with the measurement of standards of performance for specific operations, fixed or standing expenses are specifically regarded as costs which cannot be avoided by the particular enterprise entailed, if it is to retain and utilise such *facilities* of production as those outgoings warrant. It is conventional to ascribe a temporal attribute to these expenses on the grounds, as some would have it, that they are incurred quite regardless of output

---

[1] *Developments in Cost Accounting*. Report of the Cost Accounting Sub-Committee of the Taxation and Financial Relations Committee of the Institute of Chartered Accountants in England and Wales, p. 10 (Gee and Company (Publishers) Ltd, 1947).

volumes. But clearly " quite regardless " are singularly inappropriate words, for no-one in their right senses would engage production facilities unless they thought they had a reasonable chance of turning them to good account. It may so happen that they were mistaken, and it is such errors of judgment which modern accounting practice wishes to reveal as losses. It may be that the output conjecture was no more than reasonably possible, but that sectional management ability is such that drive and energy is lacking to secure what is required. This is plain ineffectiveness which the accounting art is vitally concerned to disclose. Thus the amount of output achieved in a given time is a matter of the greatest consequence to those responsible for working an operating process, for the fixed expense rate if it is to be fully recovered in all circumstances is plainly a variable depending upon the scale or level of output actually achieved. Hence, if normal output standards are set for a given period of account, and actual outputs fall below them, some part of the fixed expenses will not be taken up as part of the cost of the productive process, and will be thrown out as losses to be explained either by mistaken judgment or inefficiency. Accordingly that department of accounting which seeks to determine the internal effectiveness of an enterprise regards the allocation of fixed expense on the basis of temporal output as a subject of primary importance. Nevertheless, it is important to remember that in this context " fixed " is a relative term for there can be no question of expense constancy if the productive facilities themselves are extended. Familiar examples of fixed or standing expenses are such debits to operating account as those for establishment in the shape of rent, rates, insurances, and the depreciation and maintenance of buildings. So too, items in the order of administrative and drawing office salaries may be brought under this nomenclature.

Variable or moving expenses may be defined as those inputs which are *directly* related in more or less degree to operating outputs, and which are, therefore, quantitatively dependent upon output levels. It is seldom, if ever, accurate to suggest that they increase or decrease in direct and constant ratio to the volume of output, as this may be taken as implying such perfect correlation as to ignore the more general probabilities of falling and rising costs denoted by increasing and decreasing returns. There are many illustrations of so-called Break-Even charts which tacitly ignore the facts of experience by plotting costs in a straight line as if they were uniformly proportionate to sales, and the lay observer might well be forgiven for imagining there was no limit to the expansion of profit if saleable outputs could be consistently increased.

And what are we to make of that ambiguous classification—" semi-variable expense," " i.e. expense which is neither wholly fixed nor

wholly variable, but which contains elements of both." [1]   The Cost
Accounting Sub-Committee of the Taxation and Financial Relations
Committee of the Institute of Chartered Accountants resolve this
" via media " by asserting that " In practice it is often possible to
dispense with the semi-variable group, all expense being included in
either the fixed or the variable group." [2]   A precise mind cannot look
upon this view without feeling a great deal of sympathy with its aims ;
nevertheless such precision tends to lose some of its force unless we
come to relate it to varying scales of output.   There are some expenses
which though fixed for relatively small levels of output become variable
just so soon as those levels are markedly extended, and the whole
problem of the distinction between fixed and variable expenses must
be related to contemplated levels of output if internal effectiveness is
to be judged at the point of recovery of standing charges.

Other synonyms for the expressions fixed and variable, sometimes
encountered in both economic and accounting literature, are common
and separable.   Thus common costs are outgoing items of expense
which, as a matter of expediency, cannot be directly delineated to specific
outputs, either for the reason that there is no rational way of attempting
accurate separation or because, if the attempt can be made, it is too
expensive to bring it within the domain of the practical.   It follows
that separable inputs are those which can be easily and readily traced
to the promotion of specific outputs.   As we have already indicated
in the case of fixed and variable expenses, whether or not a given
outlay is common or separable depends on both the level of output
and the circumstances of the enterprise, and in so far as this distinction
can be maintained, we may regard the common costs as relatively
inescapable.

In the fact of a rather peculiar accounting use of the term " marginal
costs," when what is really meant is variable or proportional costs,
which has latterly come to the fore, it seems well to draw attention
to a more venerable classification which rests upon the economic
distinction between marginal and average costs.   In this context
marginal cost is the amount of the *increase* in aggregate costs occasioned
by an increase of one unit of output.   By contrast the average cost
of one unit of a given output is merely the aggregate cost divided
by the number of units produced.   From this explanation it will be
seen that there is a sense in which marginal costs are escapable.
Another expense distinction, to which we have already made a passing
reference earlier in this chapter, is that which distinguishes between
natural and functional costs.   Thus, natural costs are those which
find their customary place on the debit side of the financial profit and

[1] Op. cit., p. 33.

[2] Op. cit., p. 33.

loss account of an enterprise, where the expense items are classified in terms of the object of the expenditure, i.e. wages, salaries, rent, rates, insurance and such like items. A functional classification of expense items, such as is adopted in most developed methods of cost accounting, is that which gathers together under one activity all the natural expense items which the conduct of that particular activity or operating process has incurred.

We now turn to those problems which are bound up with the relevance of fixed or standing charges to inventory valuation. In the plain economic view standing charges or fixed expenses are regarded as necessarily incurred by an enterprise in providing its facilities for production and distribution. Once it is set up with those facilities it is bound to face such expenses irrespective of how many articles it does in fact make or sell. In other words they are inescapable so long as the management of the enterprise chooses to avail itself of facilities on that scale. Hence the fixed expenses are a direct retentive charge to operating account and should not be considered when it comes to the review of unrecovered costs for inventory statement. The very simplicity of the argument invites a claim on our sympathy, and there can be little doubt that it has much to commend it on that score when thought of in relation to financial accounting presentations, more particularly when we remember the dangerous ambiguities which have arisen where so-called unrecovered fixed expenses have been indiscriminately taken up in inventory valuations. The over-all ability of an enterprise to earn a conversion margin (based on its direct costs) sufficient to cover its fixed expenses and leave a profit is something we should all like to know when consulting financial accounts. Moreover when it comes to work in progress the mechanics of inventory valuation statement is made easier when standing charges are ignored, for then we can set up a *direct* operating account in which so far as concerns the *directness* of the component entries everything is on a " like " basis and the margin is strictly calculated as a conversion variable before the recovery of fixed expenses. But there are reservations. Professor Pigou writing in the rather different context of price regulation makes significant comments on the conversion relevance of standing charges, which are worth quoting here.

" It is conceivable that some reader, thinking loosely upon recent experience, may claim that competitive prices could be determined directly from the recorded expenses of converting the raw material used into finished goods. Plainly, however, in order to get the *full* conversion costs, we need to know how much should be added to the cost of material and labour for the share due, for the article we are studying, to the standing charges of the business. Given a decision about that, we can, indeed, by conversion cost accounting—the technique of which was greatly developed during the war—determine the proper price for any particular product or group of joint products;

but to proceed in the reverse direction is impossible. The calculation of conversion costs is a necessary step towards any practical scheme of price regulation. But it is a subordinate step." [1]

We cannot fail to notice from this quotation that Professor Pigou evidently looks upon standing charges as constituting some part of conversion costs, and this is a view which most internal managements would favour, but it cannot be overlooked that for some scales of output a proportion of standing charges might be ineffective, and quite clearly it would be wrong to regard this proportion as entering into the proper costs of conversion. This is a matter of great importance when we come to the preparation of internal working statements designed to test the effectiveness or ineffectiveness of particular operations, and in this connection there is plainly an inventory valuation problem. The Report of the Cost Accounting Sub-Committee of the Taxation and Financial Relations Committee of the Institute of Chartered Accountants makes mention of the matter in these terms.

" There are many occasions when all-inclusive costs (i.e. costs inclusive of fixed overhead expense) are inadequate in enabling management to solve readily many of the problems confronting it from day to day.

For example, when deciding :

(a) whether to buy a part from outside, or to make it in the factory ;

(b) whether or not to install new plant ;

(c) whether or not to take an extra order at less than normal market prices.

In considering (a) above, it will probably be unnecessary to include any sum for works management salaries and supervision in estimating the cost of making the part in the factory ; in considering (c) above, assuming that the works are operating at less than full capacity, there may be no need to add the full amount of fixed overhead expense in deciding whether a further order will be advantageous or not.

Costs compiled only on an all-inclusive basis not only become frequently discredited but also bring costing itself into discredit, as they come into conflict with empirical knowledge that marginal prices, although insufficient to cover a full allocation of overhead expense, may still be remunerative.

What is needed is a method of building up product costs which distinguishes at every stage between expense which remains virtually unchanged at whatever level (within reason) production is carried on, that is to say—the fixed expense of a business—and expense which increases or decreases directly under the influence of a changing volume of production, i.e. the variable expense of a business. It would be dangerous to eliminate fixed expense from production costs altogether ; the solution is to include all overhead expense but to

---

[1] *The Economics of Welfare*, by A. C. Pigou, p. 365 (Reprinted : Macmillan, 1946).

make a clear division between variable and fixed expense in the costing rates.

There would then be two overhead expense rates for each cost-centre ; one covering items which vary in relation to output, which would remain relatively constant as a rate in relation to the volume of work going through the cost-centre ; the other rate relating to fixed expense, which would alter as a rate in relation to changes in the volume of work. The appropriate rates can then be applied according to the particular purpose for which it becomes necessary to compile a cost." [1]

We may see from all this that in order to measure the effect of output variations it is necessary to relate standing charges to normal production, particularly where departmental or process efficiencies are in point. This necessarily involves the taking up in departmental inventory statements of allocated standing charges on the basis of a unit cost calculated in terms of a standard production. Hence we find the Council of the Institute of Chartered Accountants in its recommendations which concern the valuation of stock-in-trade making the point that " To avoid distortion of revenue results, in some cases indirect or overhead expenditure is eliminated as an element of cost when valuing stock-in-trade or, alternatively, only that part which represents fixed annual charges is excluded. In other cases, an amount is included which is based on the normal production of the unit concerned."[2] If we turn back and review this discussion we are virtually led to the conclusion that while in the great majority of cases it may be both expedient and desirable to exclude standing charges from inventory valuations utilised in the financial accounting measurement of the overall operating profit of an enterprise, yet it may be very unwise, and often in fact dangerous, to do so where inventory valuations are utilised in those management working statements which are designed to reveal the degree of internal efficiency with which particular operations or processes have been conducted. But even in the former case there is an exception.

If we revert to the special case of an enterprise engaged on a major work contract, we have to fall back on the issues raised in the discussion on the source and time of profit before we can decide the financial accounting relevance of standing charges to unrecovered costs. Thus, in the not too common case of a firm which is spending virtually the whole of its time and resources on one major contract during a particular period of account, everything will depend upon

---

[1] *Developments in Cost Accounting*, pp. 33 and 35 (Gee and Company (Publishers) Ltd., 1947).

[2] *Accounting Principles*, Recommendations by the Council of the Institute of Chartered Accountants in England and Wales, 1942 to 1946 : X.—The Valuation of Stock-in-Trade.

its method of taking up profits. If it only recognises profit at the time of actual realisation in terms of cash or its equivalent on final completion of the work, then if it chooses to ignore standing charges in its inventory statement of unrecovered costs it must make an equivalent loss if the contract remains uncompleted at the accounting date. The only conceivable loss which it could have incurred in such circumstances would be established by excessive costs, which would include such standing charges as were relevant to some possible ineffective user of production facilities. Hence, if an enterprise *is* operating in the special circumstances and following the particular convention we have cited, then the only reasonable course is to carry the standing charges appropriate to an effective user of facilities into the inventory statement of unrecovered costs, as utilised for the purposes of the financial accounts. On the other hand if such an enterprise has been taking up its profits on a source basis depending upon conversion operations, then quite plainly it is only proper to return to our general rule by virtually applying the standing charges against the direct conversion profit, and eliminating them from the financial accounting statement of unrecovered costs carried over to the next period.

For the sake of completeness it is essential to mention the important subject of depreciation, though the greater part of what we shall have to say has already been dealt with in some detail elsewhere.[1]

The conventional accounting approach to the problem of depreciation may be described in terms of

" that part of the cost of a fixed asset to its owner which is not recoverable when the asset is finally put out of use by him. Provision against this loss of capital is an integral cost of conducting the business during the effective commercial life of the asset and is not dependent upon the amount of profit earned.

The assessment of depreciation involves the consideration of three factors : the cost of the asset, which is known ; the probable value realisable on ultimate disposal, which can generally be estimated only within fairly wide limits ; and the length of time during which the asset will be commercially useful to the undertaking. In most cases, this last factor is not susceptible of precise calculation. Provisions for depreciation are therefore in most cases matters of estimation, based upon the available experience and knowledge, rather than of accurate determination. They require adjustment from time to time in the light of changes in experience and knowledge, including prolongation of useful life due to exceptional maintenance expenditure, curtailment due to excessive use, or obsolescence not allowed for in the original estimate of the commercially useful life of the asset." [2]

[1] *Social Accounts and the Business Enterprise Sector of the National Economy* (shortly to be published by the Cambridge University Press).

[2] *Accounting Principles*. Recommendations by the Council of the Institute of Chartered Accountants in England and Wales, 1942 to 1946 : IX—Depreciation of Fixed Assets.

The general point of view which is taken in this approach is that "Fixed assets, whatever be their nature or the type of business in which they are employed, have the fundamental characteristic that they are held with the object of earning revenue and not for the purpose of sale in the ordinary course of business. The amount at which they are shown in the balance sheet does not purport to be their realisable value or their replacement value, but is normally an historical record of their cost less amounts provided in respect of depreciation, amortisation, or depletion." [1]

The accountant is necessarily concerned with the interests of proprietors, and by adopting this depreciation approach he impliedly follows a course which looks both to the maintenance of money capital expended on fixed assets, and the eventual recovery of all money costs out of revenues by way of the operating accounts. This practical solution was developed during a period of relatively stable prices, and historically it is not difficult to show that it was partly bound up with a legal insistence on the preservation of such money capital as was contributed to an enterprise by its proprietors. There is little that we should need to say about this if we still lived in times of relatively stable money values. As things have turned out, particularly in the face of rising prices, it is very doubtful whether this traditional accounting approach can be supported   The whole question takes on a different cloak as soon as we look beyond the monetary aspects of proprietorship capital, and dividend distributions, to the means of safeguarding productive capacity by way of the maintenance of tangible assets ; for then we begin to discern a measurement of profit which does not disregard variations in *real* resources while concentrating upon variations in monetary claims.

When we regard the matter from this standpoint, we see that for a continuing enterprise it is the function of depreciation accounting to provide resources adequate to the maintenance of *real* assets. Thus, in each year, the sum of money allocated to depreciation in the operating account should accumulate in a fund which eventually proves sufficient to enable the depreciated asset, as soon as it becomes either worn out or obsolete, to be *replaced* by some reasonably equivalent asset.

Wear and tear by operational user, deterioration through time, and obsolescence take place quite independently of money values. Nevertheless for the purposes of book-keeping and accounting statement, it is necessary periodically to attach some monetary value to these happenings. The orthodox accounting methods constitute a backward-looking approach. Thus, they almost invariably reach back to historical or first (asset) costs for their value assessments of current depreciation. The economic method is a more forward-looking view for the reason that it endeavours to measure depreciation

[1] *Ibid.*

by reference to last known or current (asset) costs. No one can doubt, however, that the practical attempt to measure anticipated replacement costs of fixed assets within the period of their useful lives does present a number of awkward problems, although as is always the case with comparatively new conceptions some of the difficulties are over-exaggerated. At periodical accounting dates when the question of depreciation falls to be considered, the sensible approach would seem to require at least some reference to current or last replacement costs as better indicative of eventual replacement costs than original costs. This is particularly relevant in a period in which prices are steadily rising. Although it may be difficult to determine the current replacement cost of particular items of equipment, nevertheless it should prove possible to arrive at a reasonable approximation for main groups of fixed assets, if necessary by reference to statistical compilations of the periodical costs of capital goods.

Moreover, it should not be overlooked that in times of relatively temporary variations in prices, whichever way they go, it is probably better to have regard to the *general trend* of replacement costs rather than place too great an insistence on the last costs known at the accounting date. Again, a situation will often arise in which a business will not replace its worn out equipment with something which is exactly the same. More commonly, perhaps, it will take on new and sometimes possibly cheaper, forms of equipment contrived to fulfil similar functions more effectively. Much will depend upon the relevance of the immediate cost of the new asset to the historical cost of the old asset, but in so far as the preservation of the money claims of the proprietors of the business is concerned, it seems clear that fixed asset cost recoveries by way of operating accounts should not fall below allocations based on the money expended as capital on the original asset. At the same time it does seem that there is an esoteric sense in which it is possible to urge that the purchasing power in real terms which was equivalent to the money cost of the original asset at the time of its acquisition, should be stabilised, in which case depreciation might be validly provided on the basis of the trend of *general* price levels at accounting dates.

A troublesome issue presents itself as soon as we come to consider past depreciation provisions virtually brought forward, because the time for asset replacement has not yet arrived, at the beginning of the accounting period brought into retrospect. It raises the question of the adequacy or otherwise of accumulating replacement funds when judged in the light of the last costs regarded as relevant in the last period of account. Thus, while the current economic provision is sufficient for attribution to the operating account of the current period, the store of back provisions accumulating in the replacement fund may, at first sight, appear as out of line unless brought up to date by some adjusting reservation. The precise assessment of such an adjustment, if it be necessary at all, is a matter of some conjecture, although the guiding considerations themselves are reasonably clear. The problem turns upon the manner of investment of the replacement fund. If this fund is retained in liquid resources held in the form of monetary claims then in a period of rising prices these resources will suffer depreciation in real terms, which means that they will be inadequate to cover financially rising asset cost values. On the other hand, if, as may be, the replacement fund has been virtually invested in different classes of real assets, then it is quite possible that the last cost values of such assets will not in every case move in step with a change in the general level of prices. Some classes of assets may very well vary disproportionately and this situation might also give rise to some inadequacy when accumulating back depreciation provisions are compared with present requirements. Nevertheless in so far as such inadequacies *can* be reasonably measured they should, in principle, be made good by appropriate non-operating charges in the current revenue account of the enterprise. As a commentary on this position it also seems well to point out that, if the attempt *is* made to portray fixed asset values in the balance sheet by reference to last cost values, as finally seems the only logical stand, then such variations will involve capital surplus adjustments. But this leads us on to a fundamental minimum financial accounting obligation imposed by the generally accepted legal necessity to satisfy monetary claims in terms of money tender. In the particular context of the contributed money capital of proprietors this involves, as a fundamental minimum, the recovery of the original costs of fixed assets by charges to current accounts over the lifetime of those assets. As soon as we are prepared to admit this point of view we are forced to recognise that whatever replacement fund revenue credits are necessitated by price falls, they can never be taken below prior accumulations precedent to actual replacement, in excess of original cost.

At this stage something needs to be said about the accounting mechanics dealing with amounts provided by way of depreciation and treated as credits in a replacement fund. As we have suggested the method of arriving at the current provision in terms of last cost is to revalue the fixed assets by applying a coefficient, based on last cost, to the original cost according to the year of purchase. This is a method which has already been resorted to on the continent. The current provision is then calculated in terms of the new values of the fixed assets. This method is reasonably plain and straightforward but the time will come when actual replacement of a particular asset will take place. The amount standing in the replacement fund will virtually comprise original cost allocations plus periodical excess provisions, unless these excess provisions have been utilised by credit to revenue in a period of falling prices. We have already argued that, having regard to existing constraints, no replacement fund can be measured at less than original cost allocations. On the assumption that excess provisions of the order we have mentioned do remain in the replacement fund at the time of actual replacement, then it is clear that at that point these excess provisions have been taken up. In other words, the immediate liquid resources, answering that part of the replacement fund attributable to the particular asset replaced, have been utilised by conversion into a new fixed asset. In these circumstances the excess provisions take on the form of new money capital employed. If they had not been covered out of the current operating accounts of the enterprise, they would have had to be provided by the introduction of new money or by a draft on retained resources. Hence these excess provisions should now be transferred to capital reserve. If on the other hand, as eventually seems conceivable, fixed assets are taken into balance sheets at their last costs instead of at a variety of original costs, then it is clear that the capital reserve will require to be adjusted for the changing values at accounting dates. In these circumstances replacement funds should be brought in line with the last stated costs of fixed assets and no later transfer to capital reserve will be required at the time of actual replacement in the manner which we have indicated ; such a transfer is only needed where following accounting convention fixed assets are still retained in the balance sheet at their original costs.

We have already referred to the difficulty encountered when we come to look at back provisions and we have suggested the lines on which a solution might be worked out. It should be noticed, however, that it assumes a stabilised real capital structure, and does not seek to deal with any expansion, principally on the grounds that such a course is clearly a matter to be met either by the introduction of new capital or by the retention of profits. The principles which we have enunciated are therefore only concerned with the maintenance of original real capital and if productive facilities are increased their maintenance is only required after the point at which they have been financed. Thus current provisions will be adequate in so far as they are invested in asset resources which are similarly preserved in real terms. It is mainly when they are left in the form of monetary claims that they will suffer depreciation in a period of rising prices, as a result of which the current account will fall to be burdened with a non-operating charge to counterbalance the depreciating replacement cover. It is sometimes objected that such a course as is here put forward protects equity investors at the expense of purely rentier or fixed money capital and interest investors. In a period of rising prices this may well be true, and if it is thought that such a disparity is socially inequitable then a technical manœuvre can be quite easily arranged whereby such excess replacement provisions as an enterprise has in fact provided out of current working accounts can stand in a separately earmarked non-distributable capital reserve. Moreover, if the taxation authorities can be persuaded to allow such excess provisions as a deduction from assessable profits, then the amount so standing to the credit of this special account might very well be treated as a deferred taxation reserve to be suitably released to the authorities when the enterprise ceases to employ the facilities which such replacement provisions have covered. It is understood that such a view of the matter has already been followed in some countries.

Another argument with which we are required to deal asserts that where a number of persons have engaged themselves in a purely money venture, then at the close of that venture they are entitled to the return of the money which they have either introduced or accumulated in the venture. In such a case there can be little question that original cost allocations are properly chargeable to the operating account of the venture. This case, however, is distinguishable from that of the continuing enterprise. The necessity to replace or maintain *real* assets has no essential validity in the purely monetary venture. But it is difficult to see how a *continuing* enterprise can make profit if in point of fact the *real* assets or their equivalents with which it enters upon an accounting period are liable to be virtually depleted at the end of that period. That is to say it must end up the period with the same potential productive facilities as it began with before it can assess any net increase in assets as profit. We have repeatedly drawn attention to the observation of Mr. J. R. Hicks—

" The purpose of income calculations in practical affairs is to give people an indication of the amount which they can consume without impoverishing themselves. Following out this idea, it would seem that we ought to define a man's income as the maximum value which he can consume during a week, and still expect to be as well off at the end of the week as he was at the beginning." [1]

The fundamental idea behind this concept would seem to be just as readily applicable to enterprises as to persons, and its bearing on the measurement of profit is plain.

Although it can be said that orthodox accounting convention does not altogether satisfy this economic requirement, nevertheless it seems right to give the accounting approach its due weight. Thus accountants define depreciation in relation to fixed assets as nothing more than an amortisation of money cost over useful life. They urge that depreciation charges have nothing to do with either changes in value or replacement. The sense in which orthodox accounting uses the term depreciation is therefore limited, so that when by reason of

---

[1] *Value and Capital*, by J. R. Hicks, Second Edition, p. 172 (Oxford at the Clarendon Press, 1946).

a rise in the price level the replacement cost of a fixed asset exceeds its original cost this is a separate matter quite distinct from depreciation. Thus accountants are disinclined to use the term depreciation to cover this situation, though it is difficult to see how in the case of a *continuing* enterprise the purpose of depreciation can really be anything other than replacement. And so it comes about that in the strict accounting view replacement considerations are looked upon more as questions of policy than matters entering into profit measurement. Nevertheless on either count nearly all professional accountants are agreed that any provision in excess of the original cost allocation should be separately stated in both the profit and loss account, and balance sheet. In general most of them would view such an item as an appropriation to capital reserve rather than a specific operating charge, a situation which imposes different concepts of operating profit between accountants and economists. Yet it seems plain that the orthodox accounting concept does not make for real homogeneity when we come to look at the general body of costs ordinarily charged to the operating account of an enterprise, let alone those held in suspense in the balance sheet. Nevertheless the accountant takes the view that he is mainly concerned with sums of money and that when an economic transaction is consummated by the passage of money, the latter is the essential material with which he has to deal.

It cannot be denied that there is case law which makes it possible for annual profits to be distributed by way of dividend without making good previous losses of money capital, and at least one accountant has remarked to the writer that " it would indeed represent a complete revolution were the law to provide that possible future increases in (money) capital requirements were to be provided for out of annual profits." In the context of this discussion such a comment sets the legal view in high prominence, and while it is true that the practising accountant must keep this aspect well in mind when attending to the expedient issues of his day to day duties, nevertheless the *development of principles* should not be made to depend upon outmoded sanctions because they were given the force of law at a time when so to do seemed appropriate to the settlement of the particular issues then involved. As we have remarked elsewhere it is the enlightened opinion of society which should be the forerunner of legislation.[1]

Still, when all is said and done, there are very few accountants who would take the view that increasing replacement costs do *not* constitute a serious contingency for industry. As we have seen it is their point that such a contingency is a matter of prudent financial policy. An increase in the price level results in increased money capital requirements. It can be found in a number of different ways,

[1] Cf. *Design of Accounts*, Second Edition, p. 9 (Oxford University Press, 1947).

e.g. by retention of profits, by temporary borrowing, or by taking in further contributions of money capital. For these reasons they are averse to regarding any additional provision for money capital as an operating debit before defining profits. They say, not only is there nothing in the law which requires them to follow this policy, far from it, but there is a danger of some confusion unless it is recognised that what really has been done is to increase the money capital employed in the enterprise, and that the right destination for this, if found out of profits, is capital reserve.

A somewhat similar set of issues to those described in respect of depreciation falls to be considered as soon as we are brought to face the effect of inventory valuations on profit measurement.[1] Neither accountant nor economist would deny that such valuations are of major consequence in arriving at operating results, and quite apart from any other consideration it is a matter of the greatest importance that inventories of unused materials, work in progress or process, and unsold finished goods should be both properly taken and correctly valued. In the operating section of the profit and loss account of a business enterprise the opening inventory is charged as a cost while the closing inventory is credited to carry over such unexpired costs as are not consummated by matched revenues to the succeeding period of account.

The accounting view of inventory valuation is seen from the following recommendations on accounting principles of the Institute of Chartered Accountants in England and Wales :

" No particular basis of valuation is suitable for all types of business but, whatever the basis adopted, it should be applied consistently, and the following considerations should be borne in mind :

(A) Stock-in-Trade is a current asset held for realisation. In the balance sheet it is, therefore, usually shown at the lower of cost or market value.

(B) Profit or loss on trading is the difference between the amount for which goods are sold and their cost, including the cost of selling and delivery. The ultimate profit or loss on unsold goods is dependent upon prices ruling at the date of their disposal, but it is essential that provision should be made to cover anticipated losses.

(C) Inconsistency in method may have a very material effect on the valuation of a business based on earning capacity though not necessarily of importance in itself at any balance sheet date." [2]

---

[1] This problem has been discussed at some length in *Social Accounts and the Business Enterprise Sector of the National Economy* (shortly to be published by the Cambridge University Press), particularly in the second appendix.

[2] X—*The Valuation of Stock-in-Trade* (Gee and Company (Publishers) Ltd.).

It will be seen that so far as the purely accounting view is concerned there is no necessary question of replacement. Inventories of unused materials are simply goods awaiting conversion. Work-in-progress represents partly converted goods, while inventories of finished goods are merely awaiting sale. If the latter are sold in the next period of account the difference between the proceeds of sale and the opening valuation represents part of the profit of that accounting period. Similarly if materials and work in progress are fully converted into finished products and sold within a period of account, the opening valuations plus the conversion charges of the period are related to the selling price, and again the difference is part of the profit of that period of account. The question of replacement as such does not arise in arriving at the accounting measurement of the profit.

The economic view of the matter regards profit as the difference between the proceeds of sale and replacement cost, and in the light of the resulting implied necessity to replace goods sold the accounting approach appears to be solely a financial one and therefore from the economic standpoint defective; and in certain situations quite untenable, as in the improbable case of a realisation by a continuing enterprise of the whole of its opening inventory without replacement in a period of rapidly changing prices. The economist regards the sale and consumption of goods as reducing wealth, and in his view there can be no income until this wealth is replaced, for a society which is virtually living on its stocks of goods is living on capital. The same argument is applicable to the individual continuing enterprise. Stocks of goods, whether they be unconverted, partly converted, or fully converted, are part of its real assets, and it is difficult to see how it could make a profit if, while going to some lengths to preserve its monetary claims, it did not keep up its real assets. In any case some such stocks as we have indicated are necessary for a firm to *continue its activity* and maintain its productive capacity, so that, as we have already seen when dealing with depreciation, there is a vital distinction between the purely short term monetary venture and the *continuing enterprise*.

The strict economic view of this inventory question would look to the maintenance of *all* opening stocks of goods whatever their state of conversion, but as we shall see later this is not always appropriate to the circumstances of the individual firm. Nevertheless if we take this view as it stands and assume a quantitative increase over a period of account, we can see that if this positive change is to be properly reflected in the measurement of profit, then it is necessary that it shall be valued at or near to last cost, since presumably this was the cost at which it was bought. This would mean that the closing inventory valuation in the operating section of the profit and loss account would be equivalent to the opening valuation plus the

74

quantitative increase at last cost. It is quite immaterial how often the inventory is turned over in the period since it is only the quantitative change over the period which gives rise to a valuation problem, though it may well be that some economists will feel entitled to object that in seasonal trades the accident of accounting date may be exerting too great an influence on the aggregate level of stocks, but this is largely a question of standardising the accounting periods of selected industries. Ordinarily the price difference between stocks bought and sold within an accounting period is a direct contribution to the operating margin of that period.

If there has been a quantitative stock decrease over the period of account, then the closing inventory should remain at a valuation which is consistent with the pricing basis used in the opening inventory, for in this way the quantitative decrease is clearly revealed by pegging or standardising the basis of valuation. Nevertheless since there has been a fall in quantities it is necessary for the purposes of profit measurement to cover the difference between the opening valuation cost and the last or replacement cost of this quantitative fall, in order that the enterprise may retain its financial ability to restore the quantitative amount of its opening inventory.

A little reflection will disclose that both ways of dealing with these positive and negative quantitative changes is equivalent to controlling opening and closing inventories at last cost, for in either case the difference between the closing and the opening inventories, plus or minus the entry introduced in the case of falling inventories, is the same as the change in quantities valued at *last* or replacement cost, i.e. inventory formation valued at last cost.

It must not be thought that the implications of this approach on the lines of inventory replacement are entirely foreign to professional accounting thought. A special statement by the Research Department of the American Institute of Accountants on *Inventory Reserves* has the germ of what we have been saying. Thus, under the heading of Reserves and Involuntary Liquidation we meet this significant comment.

" In the case of reserves provided in connection with involuntary liquidation of LIFO inventories, a reserve is calculated in connection with quantities involuntarily liquidated from basic stocks. Presumably the reserve is a multiplication of the liquidated quantities by the difference between the estimated price of replacement and the price at which the same quantities had previously been carried in the inventory. Inherent in this method are the assumptions that the quantities will be replaced, and at the prices used in calculating the reserve." [1]

We may observe the accounting notes of caution in the assumptions, assumptions which largely disappear as soon as we begin to hypothesise

[1] *The Journal of Accountancy*, September, 1947, p. 225.

a continuing enterprise concerned to maintain its outputs, with an accounting portrayal of both its profit and assets related to monetary symbol in terms of *last* costs. As a piece of accounting mechanics, the latter presentation involves the raising of the total closing inventory to a balance sheet valuation at last cost, which in turn imposes a capital surplus adjustment equivalent to the difference between the first or opening cost and the last or closing cost (viewed against a steady trend) of the quantitative amount of the opening or closing inventory, whichever is the less. The valuation of the closing inventory at last cost will thereafter constitute the opening inventory valuation in the operating account of the next period. While we are on these questions of mechanics, we should perhaps observe that, when inventory replacement actually takes place, the inventory reserve then taken up should be closed off to capital surplus. In view of the existing accounting necessity to safeguard contributed money capital, it is important to see that at no time the inventory reserve is allowed to become negative, unless it be for the temporary purpose of a strict measurement of operating profit. If the latter course is followed, the negative credit to operating account uncovered by positive reserve balance should be immediately counteracted by equivalent non-operating debit.

To turn back to the quotation cited, we should mark the reference to basic stocks, for this raises the question of *normal* quantitative inventory carries appropriate to scales of outputs. So far we have been mainly concerned with the maintenance of *total* inventories, although it may be that from the standpoint of the private business the opening inventory in any one accounting period was excessive. Thus the individual enterprise is very largely only concerned to provide for a replacement adjustment in its operating account at the time when its closing inventory has fallen below that which its management regards as the normal level having regard to its declared scale of output. While it is highly probable that the practical determination of a normal inventory level is difficult, nevertheless the severance of an inventory into that part which is relatively stable, because it is necessary to maintain such an output as is equivalent to the best use of available resources, and that part which is virtually semi-speculative, has distinct theoretical advantages. It at once makes plain the dichotomy between economic and accounting conceptions of inventory valuation. In a continuing enterprise the first part has to be kept up in some real sense and should therefore be looked at in replacement terms. The second part is very largely a money profit venture and therefore a proper subject for the conventional accounting method of inventory valuation. Thus we will close our review of what is nowadays fast becoming a highly controversial issue.

We may perhaps pass on to another much disputed question which reared its head during the last war. We refer to the conception of a fair and reasonable—or, if so preferred, normal—profit. Once again, " Government Departments found it necessary to find some common denominator to enable them to assess the reasonableness of profits on Government contracts and sub-contracts. In many cases, a broad test was imposed in the following manner :

(a) The ' capital employed ' in the business was computed broadly in accordance with E.P.T. methods, subject to goodwill and accumulated losses being excluded, to buildings being valued at cost less depreciation and to plant being included at written-down value on Inland Revenue basis.

(b) The Department then computed a basic profit of $7\frac{1}{2}$ per cent. per annum on the capital employed. If the capital is turned over twice each year, the basic profit on turnover (i.e. sales) will then be 3.75 per cent.

(c) An additional percentage was then added in respect of efficiency and risk. The final figure might, for example, be 5 per cent. on turnover (i.e. sales).

The ' fair and reasonable ' profit having been computed in this way the results could be applied—

(a) In fixing profit rates on *individual* costed contracts ;

(b) In considering whether the *total* profits of the contractor or sub-contractor were excessive." [1]

Here we have a plain accounting statement of the manner in which Government Departments sought to measure fair and reasonable profits, and the first point to notice is that it virtually depended upon the capital employed theory. In this context it is clear that capital employed meant *money* capital employed since original and *not* last (trend) costs were taken as the basis of asset valuation. Thus the practical mechanics of profit control were made to depend upon orthodox accounting conventions.

For accountants it is chastening to recall in some considerable detail the comments which Professor Pigou made on this subject a fair time ago. He said—

" If then, *faute de mieux*, we decide to make use of this way, it becomes necessary to determine what rate of profit, in any particular enterprise, the price of whose product has to be regulated, may rightly be considered normal. At first sight it might be thought that this issue can be settled fairly easily. Will not normal profit be such profit that, when allowance is made for earnings of management (as in joint stock companies is done automatically), what is left provides interest at the ordinary rate on the capital of the concern ? This plausible suggestion is, however, easily shown to be very far from adequate. Let us, to begin with, suppose that the ordinary rate of interest really does correspond in all businesses to normal profits. We have still to determine what the capital is on which this ordinary rate is to be paid.

[1] *Government Controls :* A Summary for Accountants, pp. 11–12 (London : Sir Isaac Pitman and Sons Ltd., 1946).

Clearly we cannot interpret it as the market value of the concern, because the market value of a business being simply the present value of its anticipated earnings, these earnings *must* yield the ordinary rate of interest on it, allowing for the particular risks involved, whatever sum they amount to. Indeed, if we were to take existing market value as our basis, since this depends on what people believe that the system of rate regulation will be, we should come perilously near to circular reasoning. Capital value, therefore, for rate control purposes is something quite different from capital value for, say, taxation purposes. It must mean, in some sense, that capital which has in fact been invested in the business in the past." [1]

" It is usual, therefore, to make use either of the estimated ' cost of reproduction ' of the concern's plant—which may be very misleading if the relevant prices have changed substantially since the original investment was made—or of a value ascertained by direct physical valuation of the plant—the amount of which will, of course, depend on the principles in accordance with which the valuation is made . . . ; and then to make some more or less arbitrary allowance for costs of promotion, investments to build up good-will, patent rights, and so on. These *data* are not wanted for themselves, but are supposed to enable a rough estimate to be made of the actual capital investment, when this is not directly ascertainable." [2]

And lastly—

" To allow the same rate of return to companies which invest their capital wastefully as to those which invest it well plainly makes against economical production. Incidentally, if there were two competing combinations to be dealt with, it would logically require forcing the better managed one to charge lower prices than the other, an arrangement which would not only have awkward consequences at the moment but would effectively discourage good management. In this connection it should be noted that to extend combination further, so long as extension involves economies, is a form of good management, and a form that would be discouraged if prices were so regulated that no advantage were allowed to accrue to those who had brought it about. . . . In view of these complications, and of the necessary limitations of its knowledge—for, as a rule, the controllers are bound to be much behind the controlled in technical experience—a public authority is almost certain either to exact too easy terms from the concerns it is seeking to control, and so to leave them with the power of simple monopoly, or to exact too hard terms, and so, though not permitting monopoly exaction to them, nevertheless to prevent the development of their industry to the point proper to simple competition." [3]

[1] *The Economics of Welfare*, p. 367.

[2] *Ibid.*, p. 368.

[3] *Ibid.*, p. 371.

If we reflect on these several quotations we can detect twin elements in the commercial measurement of profit, which we may designate as the reward of capital, and the reward of risk-bearing and organisation. From the economic point of view there is a refinement in the distinction between interest and profit. In the ordinary run of business profit and loss accounts, it is usual to find such financial expenses as are constituted by interest on borrowed money, debited as a charge before arriving at operating profit. There is an implicit assumption in this view that the accounting measurement of profit may be related to *proprietorship* capital employed as determined from the proprietorship side of the balance sheet. In point of fact there is an accounting ratio which

" is usually obtained by comparing the net income at the close of an accounting period with the net worth at the beginning of that period. It is a ratio which in America is frequently calculated by financial journalists from published accounts and is regarded as an index of the ability of the management of a particular undertaking to earn a reasonable income on the (money) capital which has been invested in it." [1]

The economic conception of profit may be thought of in limiting terms of the reward of risk-bearing and organisation. The reward of management is properly looked upon as a cost before its ascertainment, but interest on borrowed money is excluded from the operating debits on the grounds that it properly forms part of the interest on capital employed. It seems, therefore, that there is much to be said for an accounting disclosure which would reflect the economic distinction between the reward of capital and the reward of risk-bearing and organisation. As a first start to the portrayal of this view, interest on borrowed money would be relegated, as a purely financial transaction, to the non-operating section of the profit and loss account. In order that the measurement of operating profit should conform to its economic conception, it would thereafter be necessary to charge interest on total capital employed (including borrowed money represented by operating assets, but excluding purely financial investments) in the operating section of the profit and loss account, and to carry an equivalent credit into the non-operating section of the same account. In this view the interest charge is related to the actual net assets employed in the working of the enterprise. Difficult questions immediately spring to mind as soon as we consider the rate at which, and the valuation of the net assets on which, this interest should be calculated. For the purpose of this discussion, however, perhaps we may be permitted to resolve the former problem by borrowing from the work of a modern writer on economics. " The proper procedure, if

[1] *Design of Accounts*, Second Edition, p. 18 (Oxford University Press, 1947).

we wish to isolate net profit, is to deduct from the gross return on capital the interest which might have been earned by lending that capital on good security." [1] Presumably this is a rate equivalent to the average yield on the market values of gilt edge securities at accounting dates.

The difficulties inherent in valuing the net assets employed in a business have already been foreshadowed by Professor Pigou's comments on the theory of capital employed. But surely the time must come when it is at last conceded that financial accounts, more particularly balance sheets, drawn in terms of last (trend) costs are more significant than the present type of documents, drafted as they are with money indicators of a wide variety of original and unhomogeneous costs. At least we might expect that both the quantitative expression of *real* things and the monetary claims were uniform throughout a document constructed at a defined point in time. If such was indeed the case, we might quite straightforwardly rely upon the valuation of the net assets employed in an enterprise as denoted by its penultimate (i.e. its opening) balance sheet,[2] limiting such further adjustments as might be necessary to the major capital incomings and outgoings of the period—much in the manner followed in Excess Profits Tax computations. In this way we might achieve a reasonable basis on which to calculate the operating debit for interest on capital employed.

Profit is a test of economic effectiveness, and we have sought to establish the validity of a measurement which virtually depends upon monetary flows of current incomings and outgoings, adjusted for the maintenance of *real* resources, because we think that this way of doing things, while it not only involves the least disturbance to existing accounting methods, is also as good and practical a quantitative assessment as can reasonably be hoped for to aid us in studying afresh its qualitative implications. As Mrs. Hicks has recently had the courage to remind us—

" Wherever there is freedom of entry into an industry the existence of (temporary) supernormal profits is an essential economic indicator that there is room in the industry for more labour and capital ; to tax away the profits of enterprise in such circumstances is to hinder the optimum allocation of resources. It is another matter if the excess profits can be shown to be due to monopoly control, but even then it is doubtful if a high profits tax is the most effective method of attack." [3]

---

[1] *Introduction to Economics*, by A. Cairncross, p. 271 (Butterworth, 1944).

[2] After bringing to account either proposed or, in due time, consummated distributions.

[3] *Public Finance*, by Ursula K. Hicks, pp. 227–228 (Cambridge, 1947).